Jacob Eckhard's Choirmaster's Book of 1809

Portrait of Jacob Eckhard painted by unknown artist.
Courtesy of Mrs. Allison P. DuBose of Camden, South Carolina.

Jacob Eckhard's Choirmaster's Book of 1809

 A FACSIMILE WITH INTRODUCTION AND NOTES

BY GEORGE W. WILLIAMS

 HISTORIOGRAPHER, ST. MICHAEL'S CHURCH

UNIVERSITY OF SOUTH CAROLINA PRESS

COLUMBIA, SOUTH CAROLINA

TRICENTENNIAL EDITION, NUMBER 2

THIS VOLUME IS PART OF A SERIES OF TRICENTENNIAL EDITIONS
PUBLISHED BY THE UNIVERSITY OF SOUTH CAROLINA PRESS, COLUMBIA,
SOUTH CAROLINA, ON BEHALF OF THE SOUTH CAROLINA TRICENTENNIAL
COMMISSION, TO COMMEMORATE THE FOUNDING OF SOUTH CAROLINA IN 1670.

Contents

Acknowledgments

It is a pleasure to record my appreciation and thanks to those who have assisted me patiently and cheerfully in the preparation of this facsimile edition. First among these is the Reverend Doctor Leonard Ellinwood, of the Washington Cathedral and the Library of Congress; he has been a mine of information and encouragement since this inquiry began a score of years ago. Professor Robert L. Sander, of Brooklyn College, has conferred and corresponded with me and has allowed me to consult his files at the library of the Union Theological Seminary. Dr. Irving Lowens at the Library of Congress, Mr. A. Hyatt King at the British Museum, and Mr. Brooks Shepard, Jr., at the library of the Yale University School of Music have assisted me in the examination of the collections at those institutions. To the last of these I am indebted for kindnesses beyond those of librarianship and for understanding goodwill through more than thirty years. Finally, thanks are due to Mrs. Granville T. Prior at the South Carolina Historical Society, to Miss Virginia Rugheimer and the staff of the Charleston Library Society, and to the staff of the Duke University Library.

The Reverend Messrs. Dewolf Perry and Edwin C. Coleman, rectors of St. Michael's Church at the beginning and the end of this study respectively, have been sympathetic to the investigation and have lent their interest. Grateful mention must also be made for particular assistance offered by Mr. C. R. Banks, photographer and historian; by the Reverend W. Donald George and Mrs. Paul H. Davis, organists of St. Michael's Church; by the late Mr. Samuel G. Stoney; and—most especially—by the late Mrs. Henry P. Jervey.

Members of the Perkins family have contributed their recollections and have given me information on Eckhard's descendants: Mrs. E. Miller Boykin, Mrs. Allison P. DuBose, and Miss Anna L. Nevins.

Special acknowledgment must be made to Dr. Martin Picker, editor of the *Journal of the American Musicological Society,* for permission to reprint the Introduction which appeared originally in Volume VII (spring 1954) of that journal. It appears here with minor corrections and adjustments to the text and with some new material in the notes.

I cannot conclude without a word of thanks to my associates on the Committee on Scholarly Activities of the South Carolina Tricentennial Commission and to its chairman, Professor George C. Rogers, whose friendship I have been happy to know for forty years.

Blackheath   G.W.W.
December 1, 1970

Introduction

Jacob Eckhard was born November 24, 1757, at Eschwege in Hessen-Kassel.[1] At the age of twelve he began his career as church organist by playing in reformed churches in Germany. He came to America in 1776 "with the Hessian troops, as a musician," and, after the Revolution, settled in Richmond.[2] He taught music there and very probably served as organist at St. John's Episcopal Church, for on April 15, 1786, he married Pryscilla Bryan, daughter of John Bryan, clerk of the vestry.[3]

On April 25, 1786, the vestry of St. John's Lutheran Church in Charleston agreed to offer "Mr. Jacob Eckhard in Virginia . . . the office as Clerk & Organist and Schoolmaster to the Corporation. . . . Mr. Jacob Eckhard accepted of the Office—and arrived here for that Purpose on the 25th day of September." He was engaged at a salary of £60, and received also additional fees for playing at funerals.[4] Soon after his arrival, the parish register records: "7 Februar 1787—Starb dem Mr. Jacob Eckhard ein Sohn mit nahmen Johann Georg, und würde der Abends begraben, hatt nicht länger gelebt als 6 Tagen. Würde 4 Stunden Vorher getaucht."[5]

Eckhard joined St. John's congregation and took an active part in the life of the parish. He lived on the glebe until 1790 in a house which rented for £1 per month. In 1805 his salary was changed from £60 to $214.28. In 1794, doubtless at his instigation, a new hymnal in German was obtained for the congregation, "likewise a *Choralbuch*."[6] He soon became a member of the German Friendly Society, a benevolent and social organization made up of persons of German extraction, and was elected its president in 1801 and its treasurer in 1802, which post he held until his death. In 1831, in gratitude for his services, his portrait was painted by order of the society.[7] He was also a Mason.

He instituted benefit concerts for the refugees in

---

[1] "Obituary," Charleston *Courier*, Nov. 15, 1833 (Resolutions of the German Friendly Society). The Jacob Echard mentioned in E. Milby Burton, *Charleston Furniture, 1700–1825* (Columbia: University of South Carolina Press, 1970), pp. 101–2, is a different person.

[2] "Preface" to his *Choral-Book* (Boston, 1816); Karl Bernhard, Duke of Saxe-Weimar, *Travels through North America* (Philadelphia, 1828), II, 13. I am indebted to Mr. Rogers for this reference.

[3] Register of St. John's, Richmond, Marriages.

[4] Minutes of the Vestry, St. John's Lutheran Church, Charleston, Vol. I (1759–1803), pp. 136, 143, and *passim*.

[5] "February 7, 1787—Died a son to Mr. Jacob Eckhard with the name John George and was buried in the evening; [he] had lived no longer than 6 days, and was baptized 4 hours before [his death]" (Register of St. John's Lutheran Church, Charleston, Vol. I, p. 252.

[6] Minutes, St. John's, *passim*.

[7] George Gongaware, *The German Friendly Society* (Richmond, 1935), *passim*. It still hangs in the rooms of the society on Chalmers Street and is reproduced in the *Journal of the American Musicological Society*, VII (spring 1954), facing p. 44.

Charleston from Santo Domingo in 1793, aiding them to use "their accomplishments as professions," and in 1795 and 1797 took part in various recitals in Charleston. In 1799 he and his son appeared in concert in a piano duet.[8] He was the director of the annual children's concert at the Charleston Orphan House. On the occasion of the fifth anniversary of the orphanage and the dedication of its new building in 1794, he instructed the children in singing two hymns and conducted the chorus and orchestra.[9] In 1798 and in 1806 he composed anthems for the occasion. Two hundred copies of the 1806 anthem were published by the German Friendly Society.[10]

He was the composer of two patriotic naval songs, "The Pillar of Glory," and "Rise, Columbia, Brave and Free," with words by Edwin C. Holland, Esq., of Charleston. The former won a prize in a national competition in 1813.

In April 1809 Eckhard resigned his position as organist at St. John's, applied for the post at St. Michael's Episcopal Church, and was accepted. "Many members of the Lutheran Church censured him for leaving them, but when we consider that the Organ then in the Lutheran Church was a small one, very limited in its powers, and such as was not calculated to gratify either the feelings or vanity of a good player; and that the one appertaining to St. Michael's Church was not only of great compass and power, but of an exquisite and brilliant order of tone—we must admit that the temptation was too great for a musician of such a high character and enthusiasm as [Eckhard] was, to resist. . . ."[11] His son

Jacob applied for his father's place at St. John's, but the application was rejected "because he does not possess (in the opinion of the Vestry and Wardens) a sufficient Knowledge of the German Language." Two years later, however, when a duel necessitated the incumbent's "extended absence from the State," Jacob, Jr., was accepted as organist at St. John's. He continued to hold this post until his death in January 1833, and was in turn succeeded by his brother, George B. Eckhard, who had been organist at St. Philip's Episcopal Church. George was instrumental in the formation of a choir for St. John's. He resigned in 1834.[12]

Soon after his arrival at St. Michael's, Eckhard prepared a collection of tunes, chants, and anthems for the use of the parish choir. In 1816, he arranged for a smaller collection, drawn chiefly from this volume, to be published in Boston by James Loring. This *Choral-Book* was designed for both Episcopal and Lutheran congregations; containing many of the tunes from the Episcopal manuscript, it included also an "Index of the particular metres suited to the Evangelical Lutheran Hymn Book": "The whole a selection for the service of all protestant churches in America." Common sense indicates that Eckhard began to use both of these collections as soon as they were available, and evidence from a music manuscript in the Charleston Museum suggests that the larger collection was in use at St. Michael's until after 1820. Eckhard probably used this collection until his death in 1833.

At St. Michael's, Eckhard served from 1809 to 1817 under the Reverend Theodore Dehon (consecrated Bishop of South Carolina in 1812), and from 1817 to 1833 under the Reverend Nathaniel Bowen (consecrated Bishop of South Carolina in 1818). Dehon had distinguished himself at the General Convention of 1808 by his stand in support of psalms rather than hymns.[13] He was, however, a firm be-

[8] O. G. Sonneck, *Early Concert Life in America* (Leipzig, 1907), pp. 29, 30, 36, 38.

[9] Minutes of the Board of Commissioners of the Orphan House, Vol. I, pp. 227–30. The hymns at the celebration were "Father of mercy, hear our prayers for those who do us good" (Hymn No. 28 in the 1792 hymnal under the headings "Charity to the Poor . . . To be sung by Children"; author not identified) and "Great Lord of all, whose works of Love, Creation's boundless realms display."

[10] Gongaware, pp. 30, 70.

[11] "Obituary"; see also Minutes of the Vestry, St. Michael's Church, Vol. I (1759–1824), p. 360. His name carved in the choir loft behind the organ bench is still visible. See for further information on this organ and an illustration, "The Snetzler Organ at St. Michael's," *The Organ*, XXXIII (January 1954), 134–36.

[12] Minutes, St. John's, Vol. II (1803–1819), pp. 50, 54, and *passim*. Waste Book, St. John's, p. 249 and *passim*.

[13] My *St. Michael's, Charleston, 1751–1951* (Columbia, 1951), pp. 53–54, 212–14.

liever in the value of music in the worship of the church and feared only the rise of a fanaticism which he thought he saw in the new hymns. In a sermon on psalmody he said: "It is evidently desirable, that all the congregation should be able to unite their voices in the praise of God; and to this end the tunes should be few, plain, and calculated to move them to devotion."[14] Eckhard supplied St. Michael's congregation with over 100 tunes for their psalms and hymns.

Although organist at St. Michael's, Eckhard maintained a lively interest in St. John's and remained a member of the corporation until his death. He was appointed to a committee to obtain a new English hymnal for the use of the church in 1809. He was elected vestryman in 1815–16 and served as treasurer from 1827 to his death in 1833. His final report was submitted by his son George. He was chairman of a congregational committee to consider regulations for erecting tombstones in St. John's churchyard.[15] In 1817, when St. John's built a new church, Eckhard contributed $50 to the building fund and chose pew 27. He served as chairman of a committee to receive subscriptions for the organ for the new church and examined it on its arrival in July 1823.[16] It had been built to the specifications of the two Jacob Eckhards by Henry Erben of New York, and bore a marked similarity to the organ at St. Michael's. Two concerts of sacred music on this instrument, by Jacob, Jr., are recorded in 1826.[17]

Jacob Eckhard, Sr., "the father of music" in Charleston, died November 10, 1833, having played at St. Michael's almost to the week of his death.[18] His sarcophagus, just eastward of the chancel at St. John's, bears this inscription:

This marble marks the spot containing the remains of John Jacob Eckhard. He was born in Eschwege in Hesse Cassel and arrived in Charleston in 1786. He was for 21 years Organist of the German Lutheran Church in this City and afterward, up to the time of his death officiated as such for St. Michael's. He discharged the duties of Treasurer in the German Friendly Society for nearly thirty three years with unexampled fidelity. In every department of life he was conspicuous for a rigid adherence to every principle of honor and integrity. Walking humbly before his God and being just and charitable to all Mankind, he died on the 10th November 1833 in the 76th year of his age.

A figure of no little prominence in the civic as well as the cultural life of his city, Jacob Eckhard gained the respect of all Charlestonians. His contributions—charitable and musical—marked the activities of many phases of the life of the city. His principal worth lay in his musical accomplishments. Almost single-handedly he preserved the quality, flavor, and excellence of the colonial period of Charleston music many years after it should reason-

---

[14] Theodore Dehon, "On Psalmody," *Sermons* (Charleston, 1820), Vol. I, p. 211. For the vigor of the decade 1809–19, see *St. Michael's,* pp. 53–56. See also C. E. Gadsden, *Theodore Dehon* (Charleston, 1833), pp. 106, 124–25.

[15] Minutes, St. John's, *passim.* George took his father's place as treasurer of the German Friendly Society (*Courier,* Nov. 22, 1833).

[16] The examining board consisted of members of St. John's, all of whom were outstanding in the musical life of the city: Jacob Eckhard, Sr., organist of St. Michael's; Jacob Eckhard, Jr., organist of St. John's; George B. Eckhard, organist of St. Philip's; John Siegling, founder of America's first music store; John Speisseger, organ-builder. Jacob, Sr., had served similarly to examine the new organ at St. Philip's in 1805.

[17] Minutes, St. John's, Vol. III (1818–1829), pp. 189, 206. The specifications are printed in full in *JAMS,* VII, 43.

[18] *Courier,* Nov. 11, 22, 1833. For his will, see Wills of Charleston County, Book C (1826–1834). Four children predeceased him: John George, John, Priscilla, and Jacob, Jr.; and three survived: Margaret, George Bryan, and Caroline.

It is of interest to record that Priscilla married Pierre Laurent de Jumelle, a Santo Domingan refugee, and settled in Camden, South Carolina. Their daughter Priscilla de Jumelle (m. Benjamin Perkins) is said to have been a talented musician; her daughter Caroline Jumelle Perkins (m. her third cousin Roger Perkins) played the organ in the Presbyterian Church in Camden and also taught "music and courtly manners" to young Miss Marian Nevins (her husband's niece) who became Mrs. Edward MacDowell, the wife of the composer. "The first studio built at the MacDowell Colony at Peterborough is called the 'Caroline Jumelle Perkins Studio.' " (Information supplied by members of the Perkins family: Mrs. E. Miller Boykin [the owner of Eckhard's piano] and Miss Anna L. Nevins.) Eckhard owned— probably a gift from a Santo Domingan—a copy of *Oficio de la Semana Santa* (Madrid, 1788), a music book for the Roman Catholic Offices of Holy Week; it is now in the South Caroliniana Library. It is to be doubted that he made any practical use of the volume.

ably have passed. He stands importantly as the last in a distinguished line of colonial musicians.

Eckhard prepared his tune book for St. Michael's Church in 1809.[19] The collection was designed to accompany *A Selection of Psalms with Occasional Hymns,* compiled in Charleston in 1792 by the Reverend Messrs. Robert Smith, rector of St. Philip's Church, and Henry Purcell, rector of St. Michael's Church. Eckhard's collection provides tunes for all but two of the forty-six psalms in the *Selection* (more than one tune for several) and for half of the forty-seven hymns. The significance of the book lies in the record and the collection of these tunes. They are in the best conservative taste. Though many of them are contemporary, they seldom are either the very florid English or the "fanatical" American tunes. They embrace the traditions of several hymnodies and disclose the caliber of Eckhard's abilities and judgment and the good musical taste of the congregation; they are at the same time an accurate picture of Charleston hymnody during the early nineteenth century. They derive from four general sources: local composers, German chorales, American tune books, and English tune books.

The tunes of local origin constitute the most important group of the collection, and most of them are located at the beginning of the book as if Eckhard recognized their uniqueness. There are at least eighteen tunes positively by local composers, and there are probably others. Of the composers, Peter Valton, the most gifted of the group, was organist at St. Philip's and at St. Michael's Churches in Charleston and had been deputy organist at Westminster Abbey. He was also the composer of a number of catches and glees that appeared in various London collections. In two of his psalm tunes ninth chords are figured, and generally his harmonies are richer than those of his associates. Jervis Henry Stevens, also organist at both

---

[19] For additional comment on the date, see the Notes to the Facsimile under "Signature and Date."

Episcopal churches in Charleston, was another contributor. The Rev. Henry Purcell, rector of St. Michael's from 1782 to 1802, was the composer of several tunes of the florid type popular in England at that time. His work is notably "showier" than that of Valton or Stevens, who contented themselves with the more straightforward half-note block psalm tunes of the English tradition. Several of these tunes are given local names: CHURCH STREET, ST. MICHAEL'S NEW, ST. PHILIP'S, and possibly ST. ANDREW'S and ST. PAUL'S. It is very probable that Purcell inspired the writing of these tunes, for as musician and rector he took a keen interest in the musical activity of the parish, establishing at St. Michael's the first vested choir of boys in this country. Valton and Stevens both served with him from 1782 to 1784. How many tunes of local origin have been lost, it is impossible to say, but it is fortunate indeed that Eckhard thought to preserve even these few records of the Charleston church musicians.

From the German tradition Eckhard has utilized the chorales "Kommt her zu mir spricht Gottes Sohn," "Wer nur den lieben Gott lässt walten," and, under the name LUTHER'S HYMN, the tune traditionally set to "Nun freut euch, lieber Christen gemein" or "Es ist gewisslich an der Zeit." Under deceptive saints' names or local place-names are concealed other chorales:

"Christus der ist mein Leben" is named GRANBY (a ferry and town on the Congaree River in South Carolina);

"Herr Jesu Christ dich zu uns wend" is named TRADD STREET (a street in Charleston);

"Mach's mit mir, Gott, nach deiner Gut" is named CAMDEN (a town in South Carolina);

"Nun danket all und bringet Ehr" is named ST. GEORGE'S NEW (a rural parish near Charleston);

"Nun sich der Tag geendet hat" is named ST. DAVID'S NEW (the parish for Cheraw, S. C.);

"Wenn wir in höchsten Nöten sein" is named ST. PHILIP'S NEW (a parish in Charleston).

These chorales are given in the settings that must have been thoroughly familiar to any organist trained in the Lutheran tradition.

A few American influences are to be seen in Eckhard's collection. Nine of the eighteen tunes from the proposed Episcopal hymnal of 1785 are included: ANGEL'S HYMN, BEDFORD, CANTERBURY, COLESHILL, MEAR, OLD 100TH, HANOVER, ST. JAMES'S, and ST. MATTHEW'S.[20] Two editions of *American Harmony* are represented: 1769 by BOSTON, ISLINGTON, and ST. SIMON'S; and 1793 by AYLESBURY and WELLS. Lewis Edson's LENOX, first published in 1782, is given but not in the fuguing form. This tune is probably the only one from the New England school to be included in the collection. The SICILIAN MARINER'S HYMN, first published in Philadelphia in 1794, is a good example of Eckhard's patriotism and timeliness. A few tunes may have been taken from Amos Pilsbury's *United States' Sacred Harmony,* a collection published in Boston in 1799 but available for sale in Charleston where Pilsbury lived. There are also in the tune book two interesting chants from the Moravian Brotherhood.

Properly, the chief source of the tunes was the English psalters and tune books, through which Eckhard ranged extensively. Croft's ST. ANNE's, Howard's ST. BRIDE (ALL SAINTS), Purcell's (?) BURFORD, Darwall's DARWALL's, Wesley's (?) IRISH, Lampe's KENT, Wainwright's LIVERPOOL, Francis Linley's PENTONVILLE, Nares's WESTMINSTER, and many other staples of the time are to be found. The opening lines of the

aria from *Messiah,* "I know that my Redeemer liveth," formed into the tune BRADFORD, called by Eckhard MESSIAH, are included. PORTUGUESE HYMN (*Adeste fideles*) and PLEYEL'S HYMN, the former dating in published form from 1782, the latter from 1791, and VANHALL'S GERMAN HYMN, a secular theme for a set of variations (1790), indicate that Eckhard was keeping up with his times musically. The popular orphanage singing groups and singing societies in eighteenth-century England are represented by MADAN's, a composition by Lockhart, organist at the Lock Chapel, by MOUNT EPHRAIM, used at the Countess of Huntingdon's Chapel at Bath, and by a number of psalm settings from the *Foundling Collection*s of 1774 and 1796.

In addition to the psalm and hymn tunes there are eight single chants without texts, two double chants without texts, and seven chants set to the canticles of the Episcopal church. Some of these last are given in rather elaborate choral arrangements. For morning prayer there are settings for the *Venite,* the *Gloria Patri* and *Gloria in excelsis* after the psalm, the *Jubilate* after the second lesson, and the *Grace;* for evening prayer, settings for the *Gloria Patri,* the *Deus misereatur* and *Benedic, anima mea* after the second lesson, and the *Grace;* for Holy Communion, settings for the acclamation before the Gospel and for the *Gloria in excelsis.* The grace is from the Moravian Brotherhood, and one chant is from the proposed hymnal of 1785.

There are five anthems and several hymns in special choral settings. Two of the anthems are probably original with Eckhard and may have been written for the Charleston Orphan House. Two hymns are from Madan's *Lock Collection* (1769): DENBIGH, to which is set Addison's "The spacious Firmament on high," and DENMARK, to which is set "Before Jehovah's awfull Throne." The Easter hymn, "Jesus Christ is risen today," is from the *Foundling Collection* of 1774. There is one Christmas anthem by Linley and another by Capel Bond, both published in London, the former in 1790. A

---

[20] Of the original eighteen of these 1785 tunes, seven have demonstrated their value and durability by surviving nearly 200 years of congregational singing and are still in regular use in the Episcopal church (in *The Hymnal 1940*). As an indication of Eckhard's intelligence and sound taste, it should be observed that all of these seven are included in the nine which Eckhard copied into his tune book: 6, 9, 37, 38 (not in 1940), 39, 47 (not in 1940), 55, 67, 81. The first three tunes in 1785—*St. James's, Canterbury, Coleshill*—appear in the same sequence in Eckhard's tune book—37, 38, 39—a good argument that Eckhard was copying them directly from the 1785 collection. In addition to the seven tunes deriving from 1785, the following tunes in Eckhard's collection also are in *The Hymnal 1940*: 12, 16, 17, 31, 41, 53, 60, 61, 76, 82, 85, 87.

rousing patriotic anthem for the Fourth of July concludes the collection.

The Reverend Dr. Leonard Ellinwood has described the manuscript as

a fascinating summary of the creative musical activity at St. Michael's over several generations. Performed by its vested boy choir, this was unquestionably the finest music in any church in the country. Not only was this true in the matter of repertory and performance, but even more so in its liturgical correctness and taste. The entire establishment reflects the conscientious work of clergy, vestry, and musicians to a degree not observed elsewhere.[21]

---

[21] Leonard Ellinwood, *The History of American Church Music* (New York, 1953), p. 89.

The Facsimile

[This facsimile includes all parts of the manuscript choirmaster's book except the endpapers and the inside back cover, all of which are blank. Modern folios have been supplied in the upper outside corners of each page, and modern numbers and letters identifying the unnumbered tunes, chants, and anthems have been placed in the outside margins where appropriate. In the Notes to the Facsimile these numbers and letters are enclosed in brackets to indicate that they are editorial additions.]

3

NOTICE.

The Members of the Choir are particularly requested not to *write in*, *turn over* the backs, or otherwise deface the Manuscript Books—They were made with much cost of *time*, labour and expense, and belong exclusively to the Organist.

Any Member of the Choir will have the priviledge to take home to practice from, any book or books—provided they notify the Organist of the same, who will enter such, in a memorandum book kept for that purpose.

N. B. All borrowed books must be returned on the following Sunday morning.

The Organist

Shall perform the duties of his Office, which shall from time
to time be directed by the ministers, in the mornings & evenings
of every Sabbath day in the year; also on such festivals or
Holy-Days, as now are, or shall hereafter be established by
the said Church, and at such other periods as shall be
appointed by authority: He shall perform on the Organ,
at all times preceding the services of the day, the tune
usually adapted the 36 Hymn, or any other solemn piece
of music; to begin at the exact time the clergyman enters
the desk, and to continue the music for one verse only
or for a reasonable time. He shall chaunt the "venite exulte-
mus" and te Deum, on alternate Sundays; and shall play
a solemn & well adapted Voluntary preceding the first lesson,
and shall receive from the Clerk such psalms or hymns,
as the ministers shall appoint for the day, in order to adapt
them to suitable tunes. He shall not only accompany
the clerk with the Organ, in such psalms & hymns as
may be appropriated by the ministers; but shall join the
Clerk in the Gloria Patri, which shall invariably be sung after
ev'ry Sermon: He shall also perform at all funerals, to which
he may be invited, accompanying the clerk with the Organ
in the Gloria Patri, which shall always be sung at the
conclusion of funerals, psalms or hymns: He shall, in
conjunction with the clerk, instruct such youth as chuse
to attend, who shall be particularly placed under his charge
in the rules & practise of psalmody; and he shall command
and require of them, a serious & decent deportment, during
time of divine service: And at the conclusion of the morning &
evening service, the Voluntary, which he shall play, shall be some
piece of sacred music, of rather slow time, such as will tend to
cherish the solemn impressions made by the pious exercises of
prayer & exhortation. And lastly, it is fully understood & required
that he shall be under the direction of the clergymen of the said
Church for the time being, in all things appertaining to its religious
service.

6

0.1 L. M.   Portugal

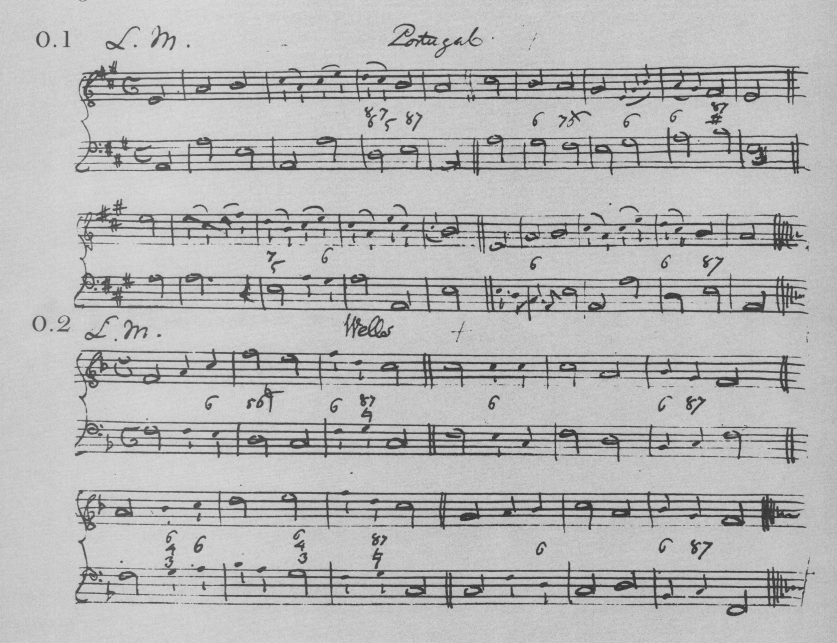

0.2 L. M.   Wells   +

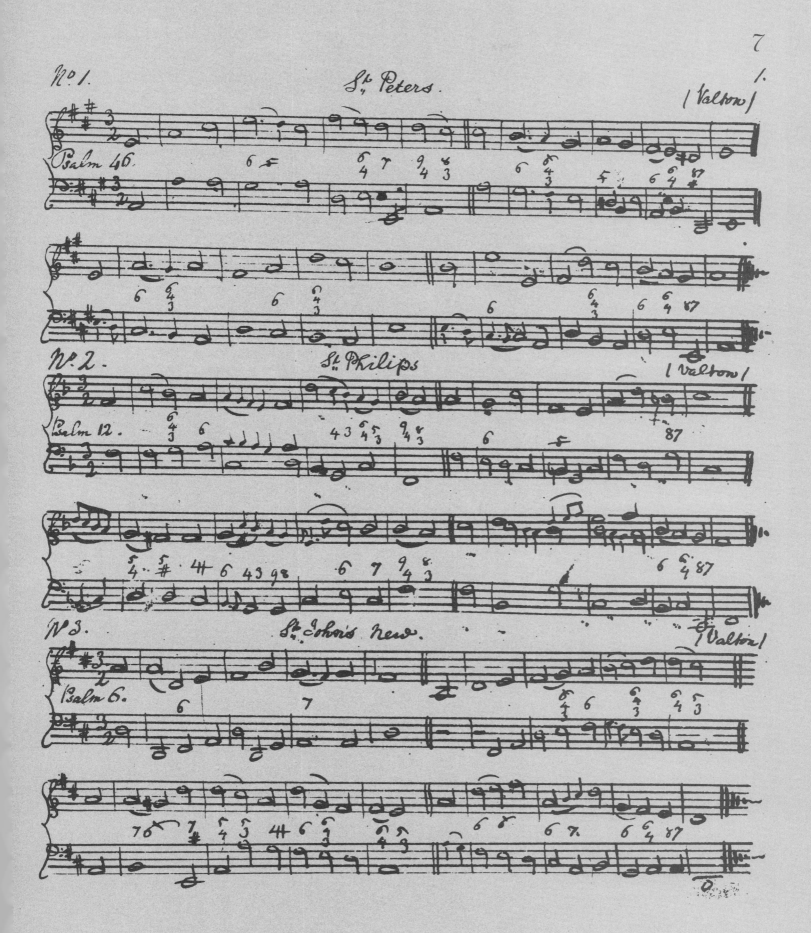

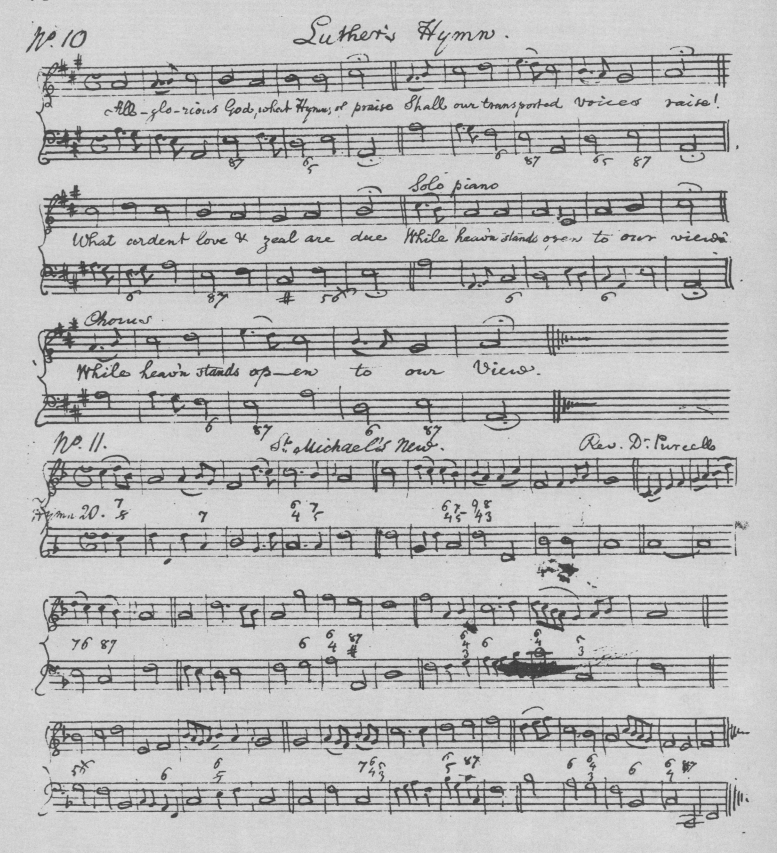

Nº 10   Luther's Hymn.

All-glo-rious God, what Hymns of praise Shall our transported voices raise!

What ardent love & zeal are due While heav'n stands open to our view.

Solo piano

Chorus

While heav'n stands op—en to our view.

Nº 11   St. Michael's New.   Rev. Dr. Purcell

Hymn 20.

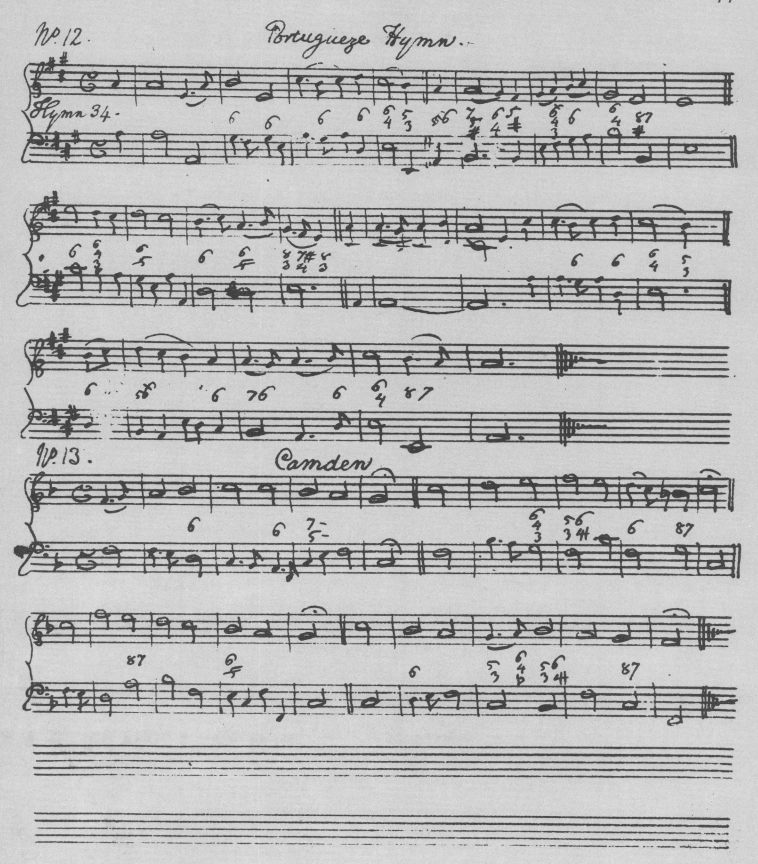

Nº 12.   Portugueze Hymn.

Hymn 34.

Nº 13.   Camden

11

12

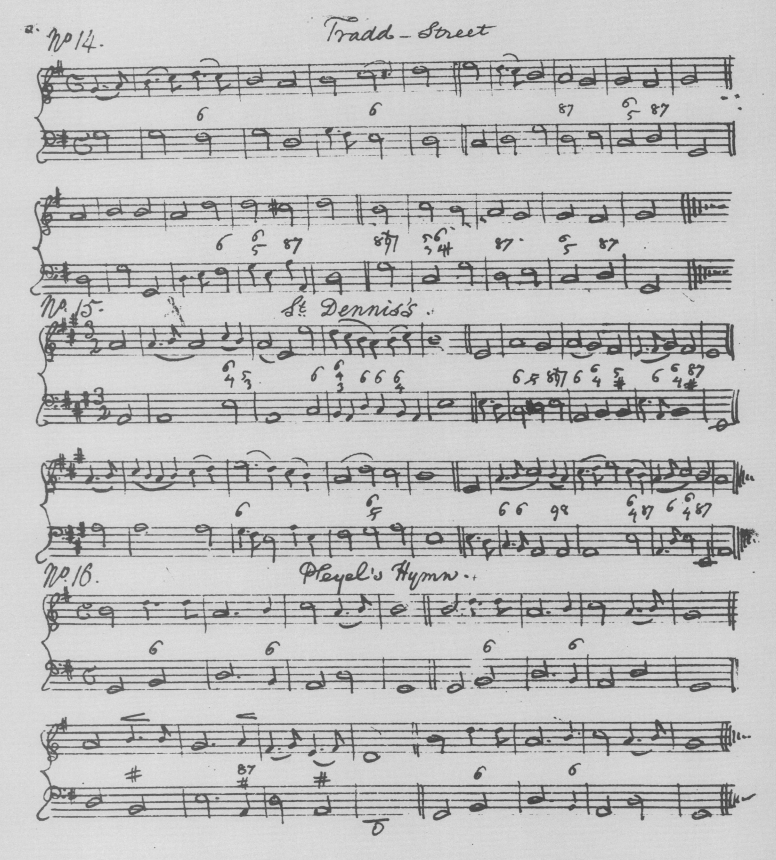

Nº 14.   Tradd-Street

Nº 15.   St. Denniss.

Nº 16.   Pleyel's Hymn.

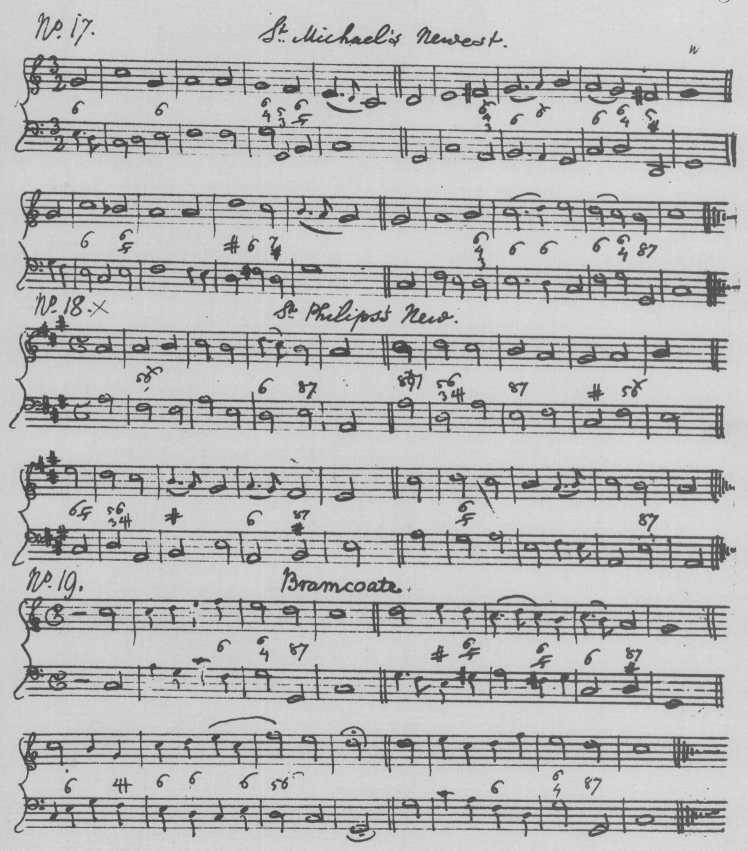

No. 17.   St Michael's Newest.

No. 18. ✗   St Philips's New.

No. 19.   Bramcoate.

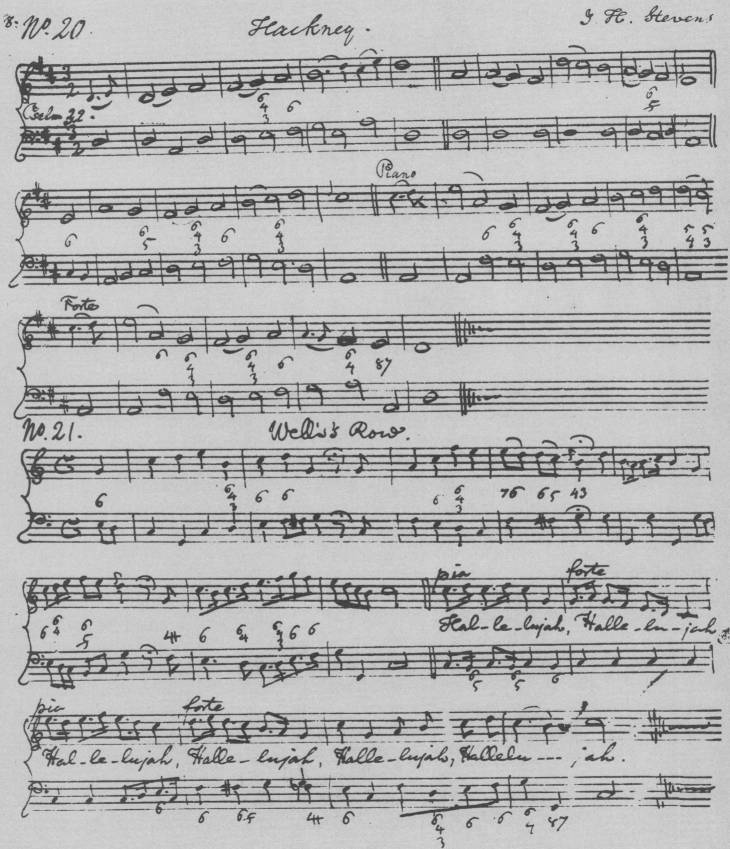

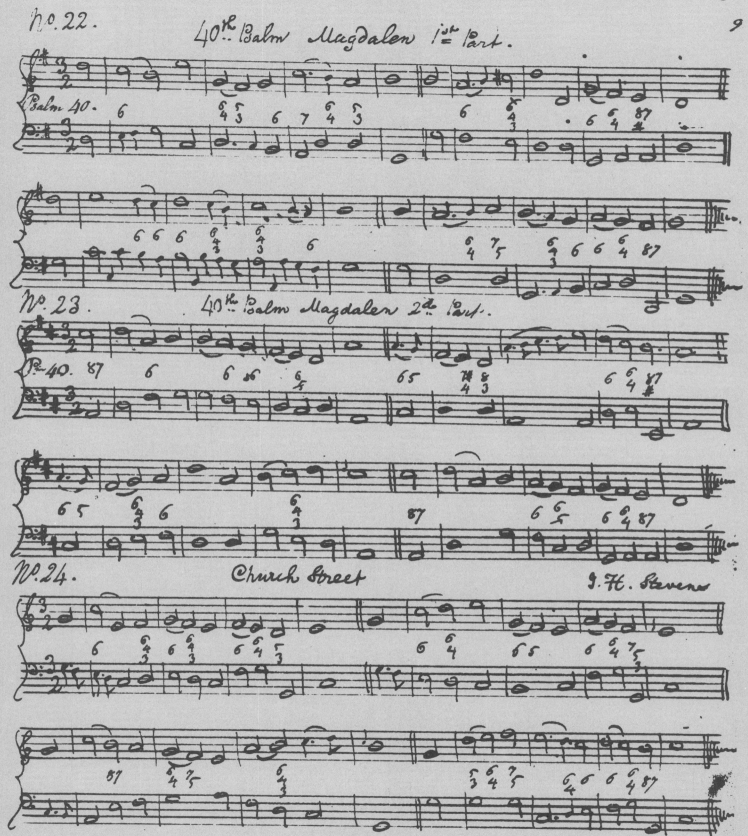

No. 22. 40th Psalm Magdalen 1st Part.

No. 23. 40th Psalm Magdalen 2nd Part.

No. 24. Church Street J. H. Stevens

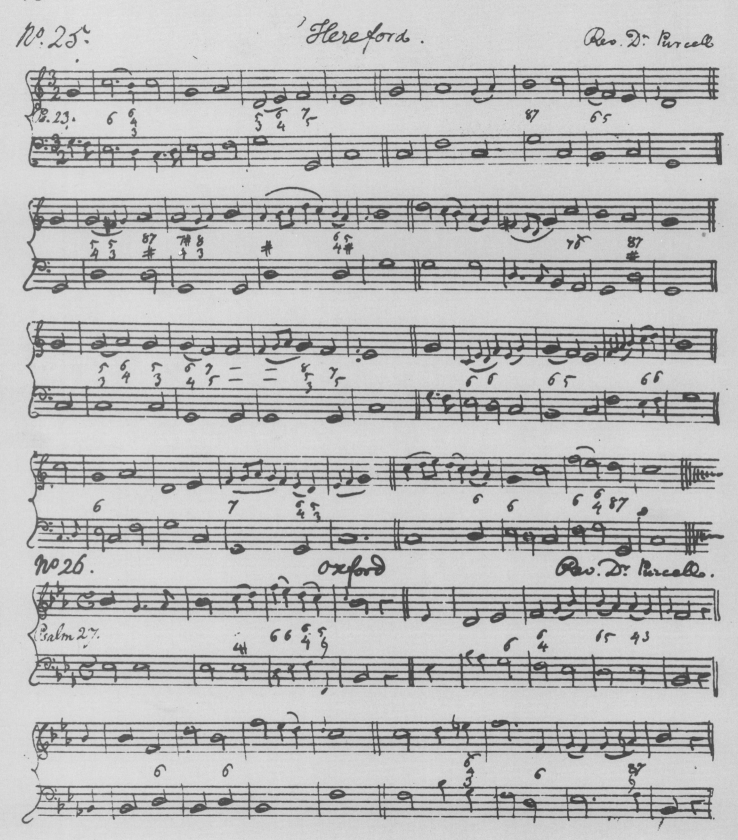

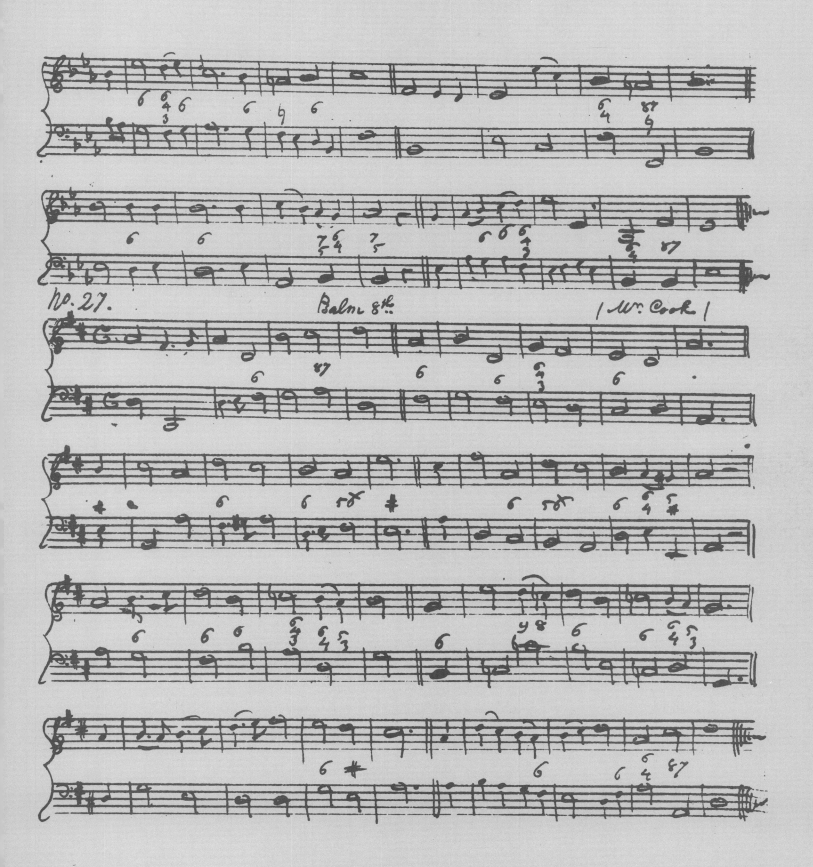

N⁰. 27.   Balm 8th.. | M͞r. Cook |

18

No. 28.   Denbigh.

Hymn 31.

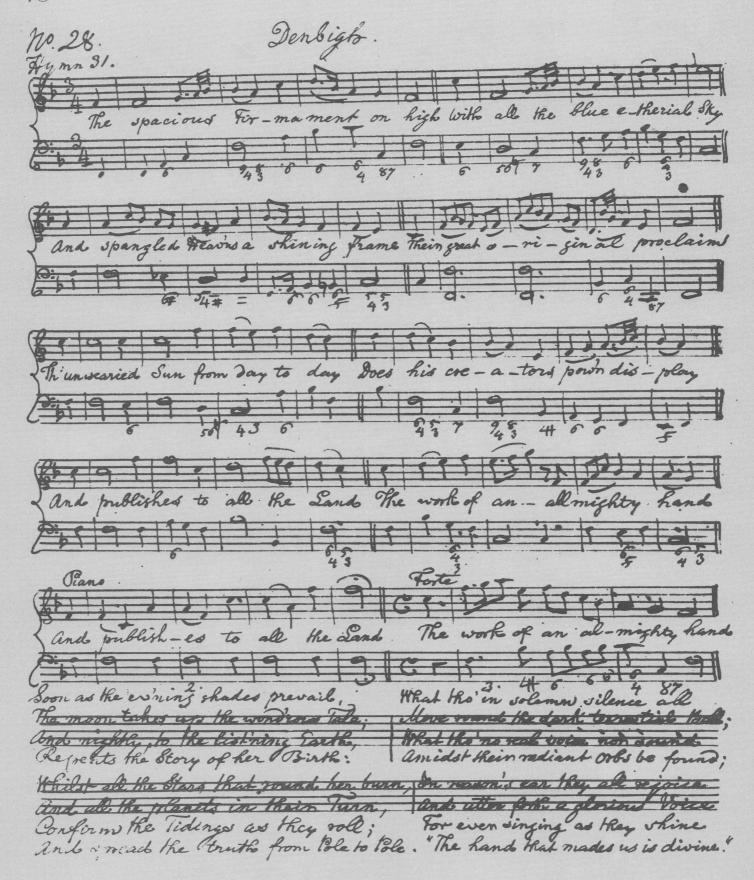

The spacious Fir—ma ment on high with all the blue e—therial Sky

And spangled Heav'ns a shining frame Their great o—ri—gin al proclaim

Th' unwearied Sun from day to day Does his cre—a—tors pow'n dis—play

And publishes to all the Land The work of an— all mighty hand

Piano   Forte

And publish—es to all the Land   The work of an al—mighty hand

Soon as the ev'ning shades prevail,   What tho' in solemn silence all
The moon takes up the wondrous Tale,   Move round the dark terrestrial ball;
And nightly to the list'ning Earth,   What tho no real voice nor sound
Repeats the Story of her Birth: Amidst their radiant Orbs be found;
Whilst all the Stars that round her burn,   In reason's ear they all rejoice
And all the planets in their Turn,   And utter forth a glorious Voice
Confirm the Tidings as they roll;   For ever singing as they shine
And spread the Truth from Pole to Pole.   "The hand that made us is divine."

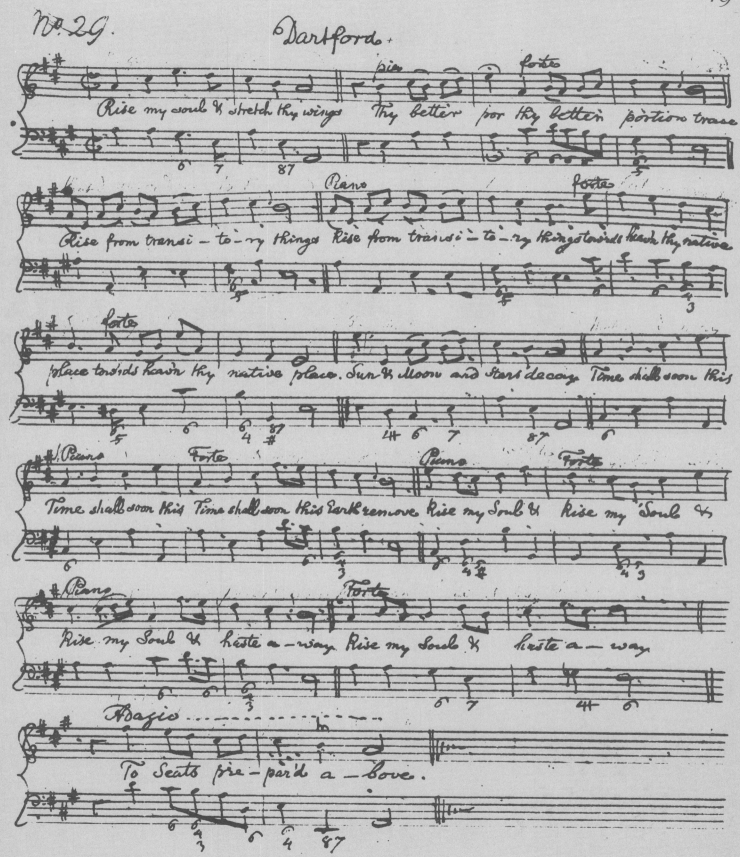

No 30.
Hymn 36.

Denmark

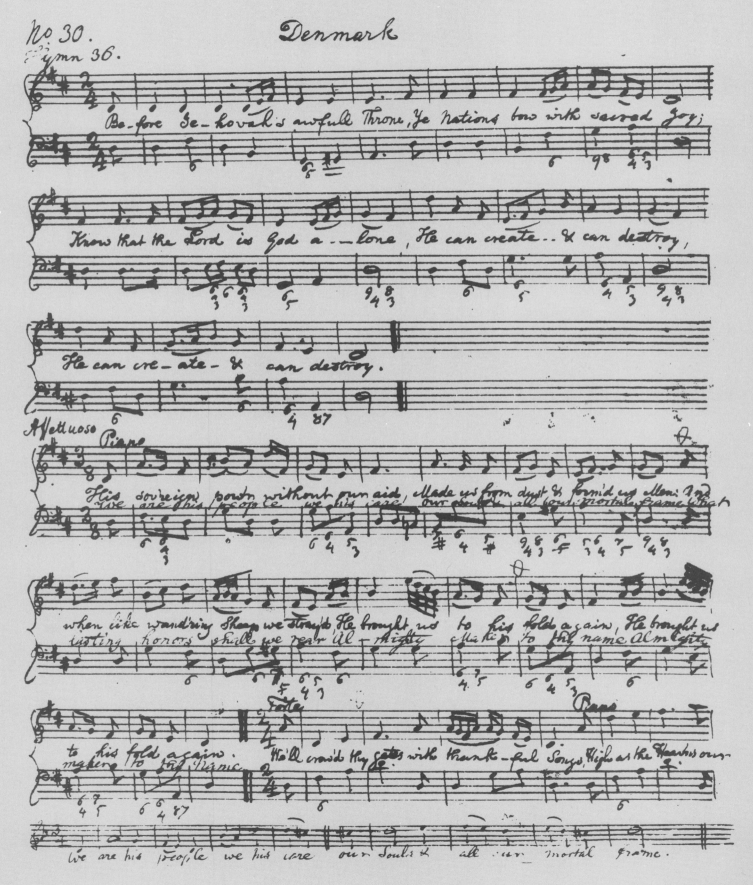

Be-fore Je-hovah's awfull Throne, Ye Nations bow with sacred Joy;

Know that the Lord is God a—lone, He can create.. & can destroy,

He can cre—ate— & can destroy.

Affettuoso Piano

His sovreign power without our aid, Made us from dust & form'd us Men: And
we are this people, we his care! our souls & all our mortal frame what

when like wand'ring Sheep we stray'd He brought us to his fold again, He brought us
lasting honors shall we rear Al—mighty Maker to thy name Almighty.

to his fold again. We'll crowd thy gates with thank—ful Songs, High as the Heavens our
makers to thy name.

we are his people we his care our souls & all our mortal frame.

22

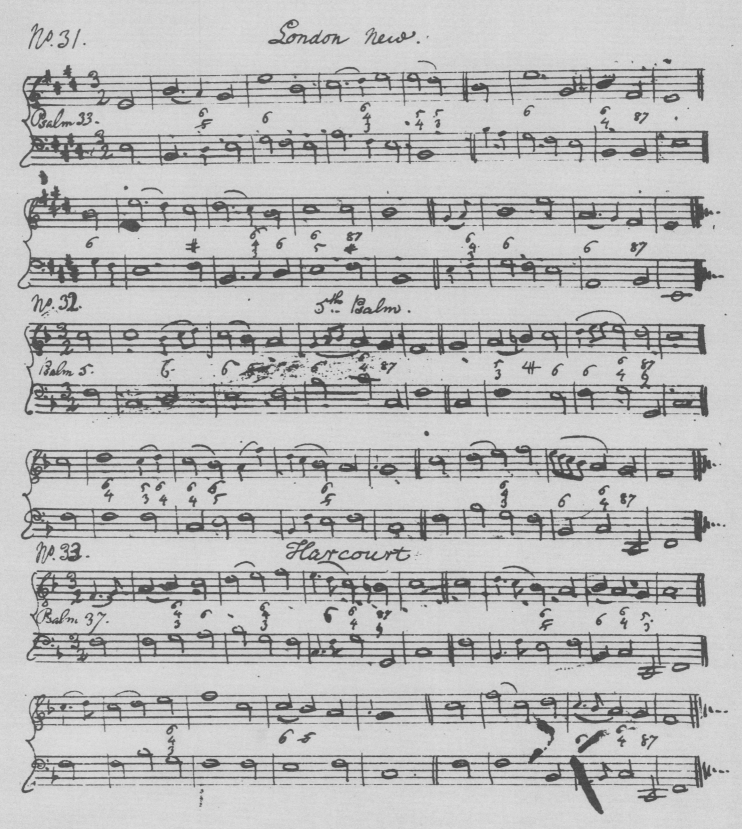

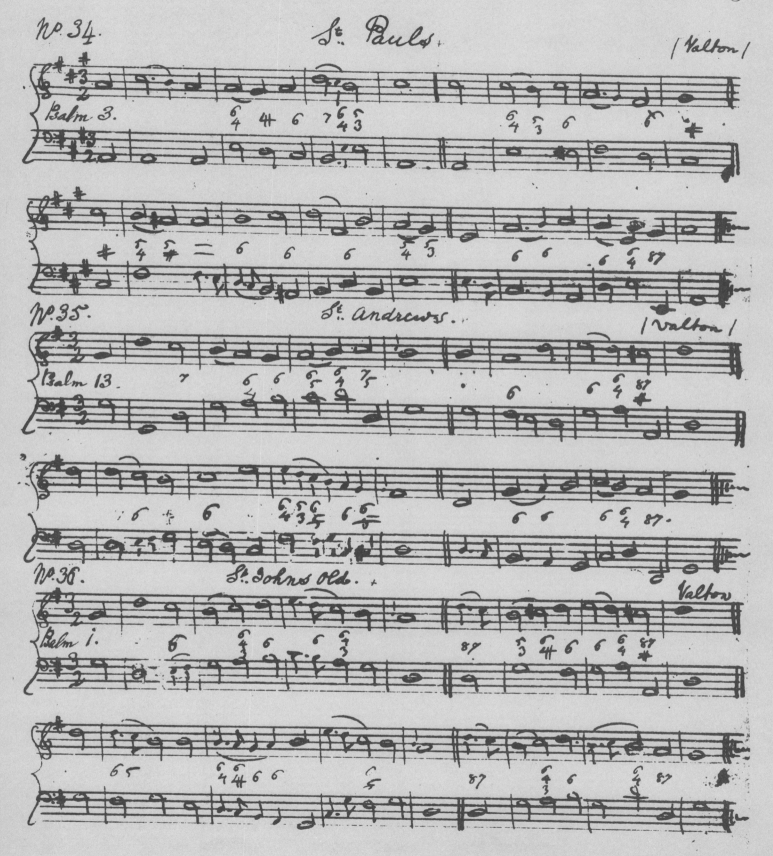

No. 37.   St. James's.

Psalm 11.

No. 38.   Canterbury

No. 39.   Coleshill

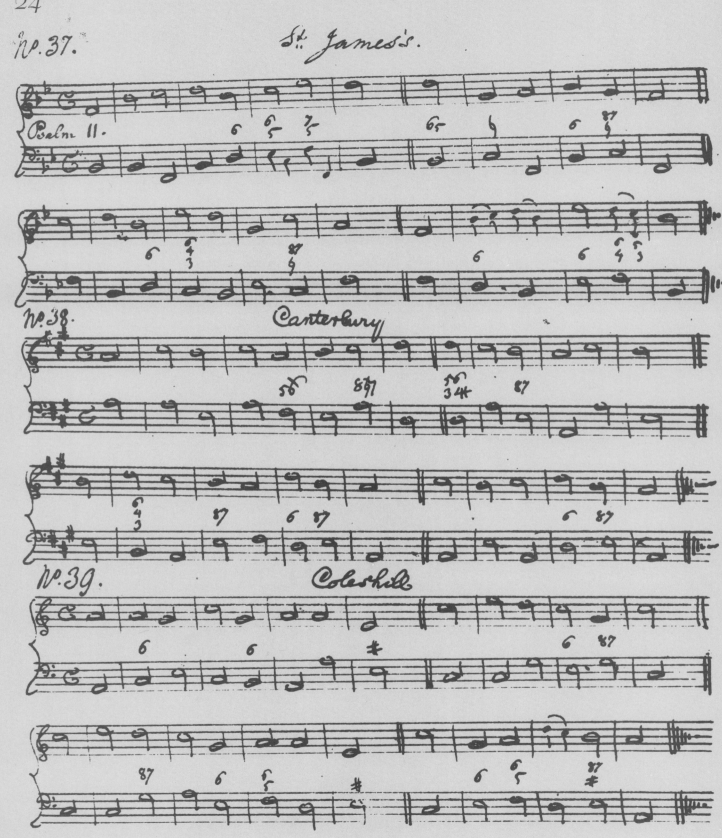

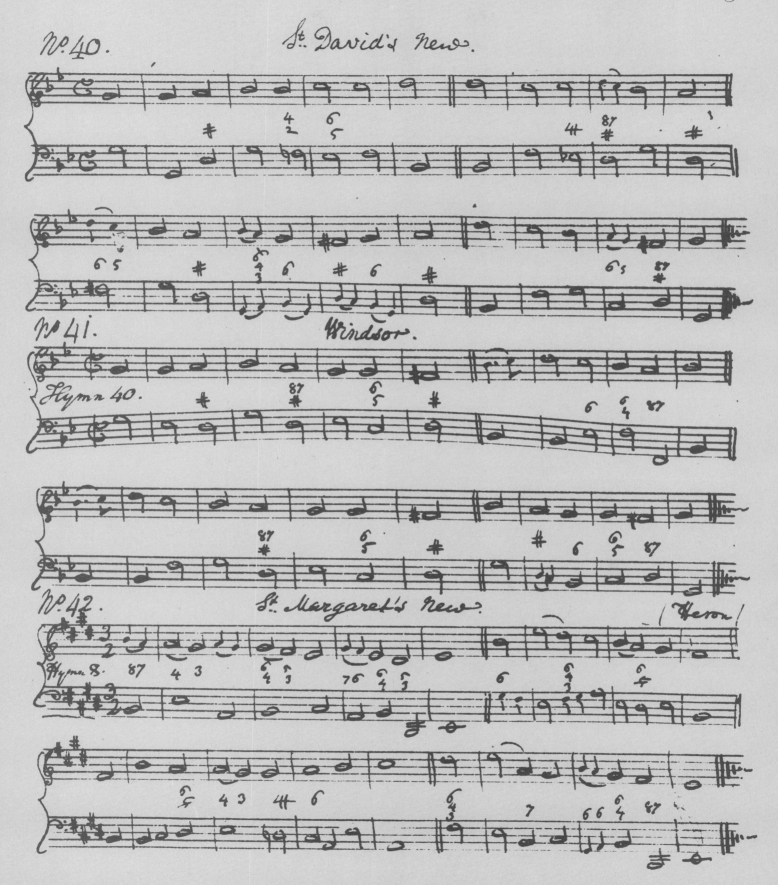

No 43.   Bexly

No 44.   Crowle.

No 45.   Liverpool.

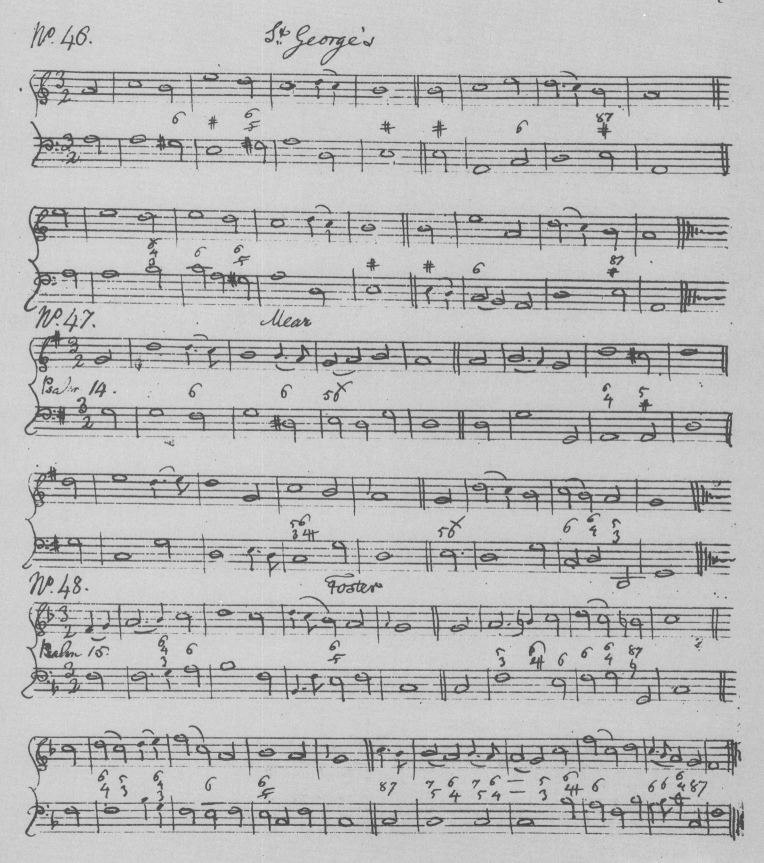

Nᵒ. 46.   St George's

Nᵒ. 47.   Mear
Psalm 14.

Nᵒ. 48.   Foster
Psalm 15.

No. 49.

Poplar

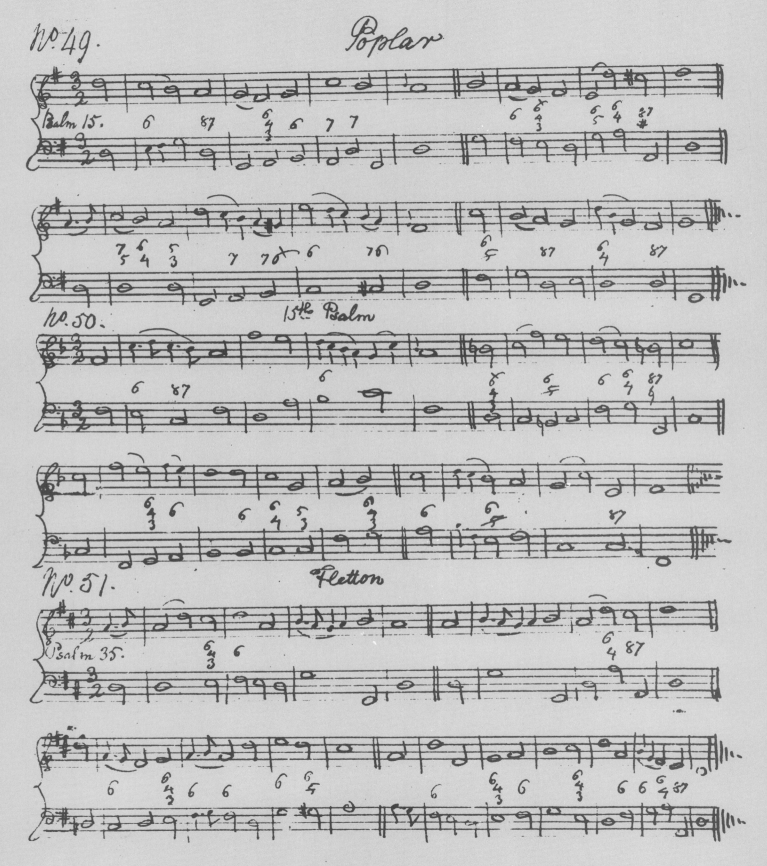

No. 50.

15th Psalm

No. 51.

Fletton

No. 52.

Christ Church

No. 53.

St. Ann's old.

No. 54.

Amesbury

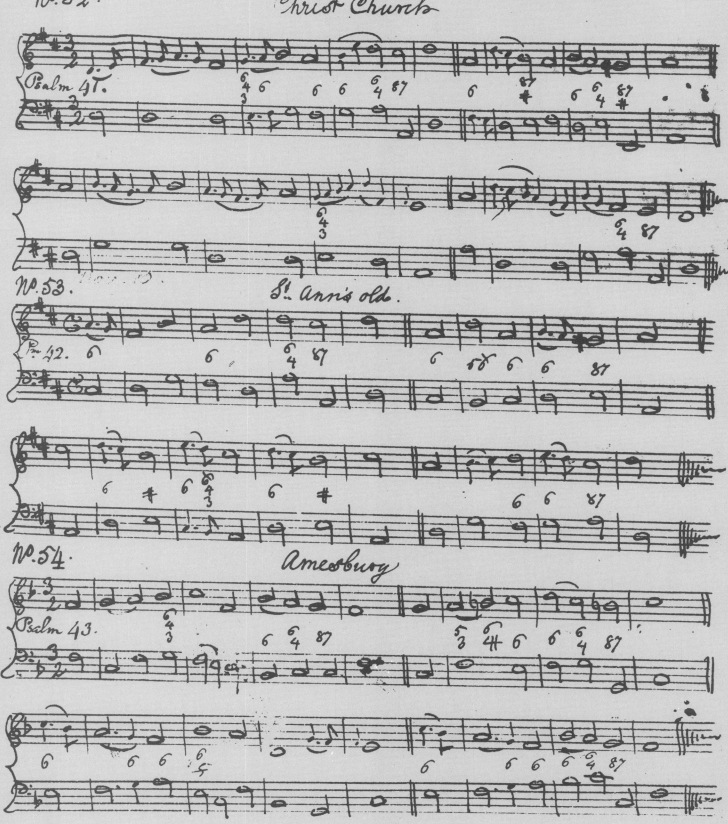

Nº 55. Bedford

Psalm 20.

Nº 56. Messiah.

Nº 57. Newark

Hymn 22.

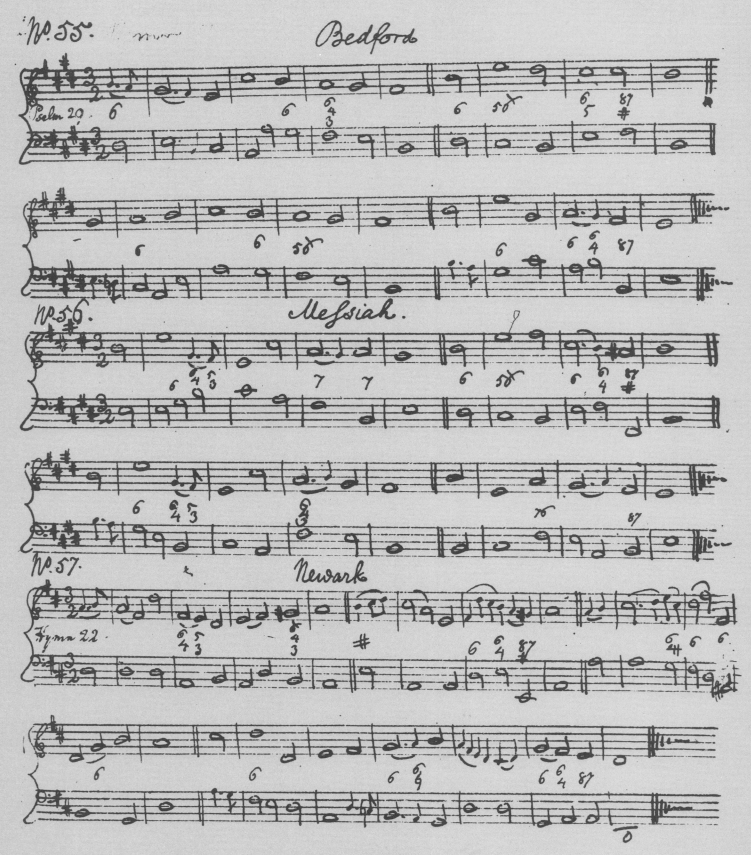

Nº 58.   Westminster

Nº 59.   Granby.

Nº 60.   St. George's new.

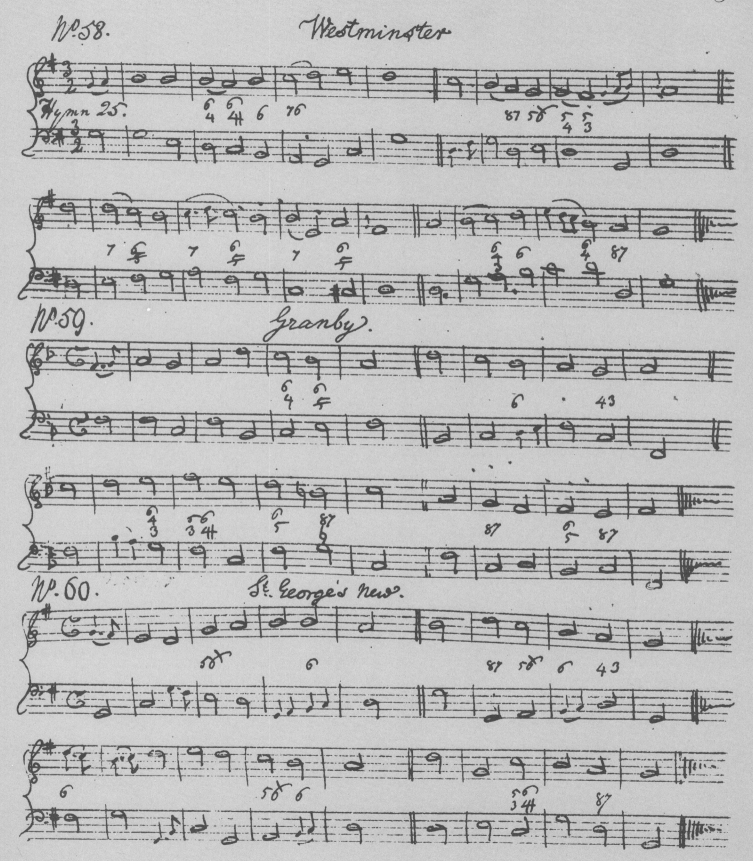

Nº 61.   Irish

Nº 62.   Abingdon

Nº 63.   Psalm 23.

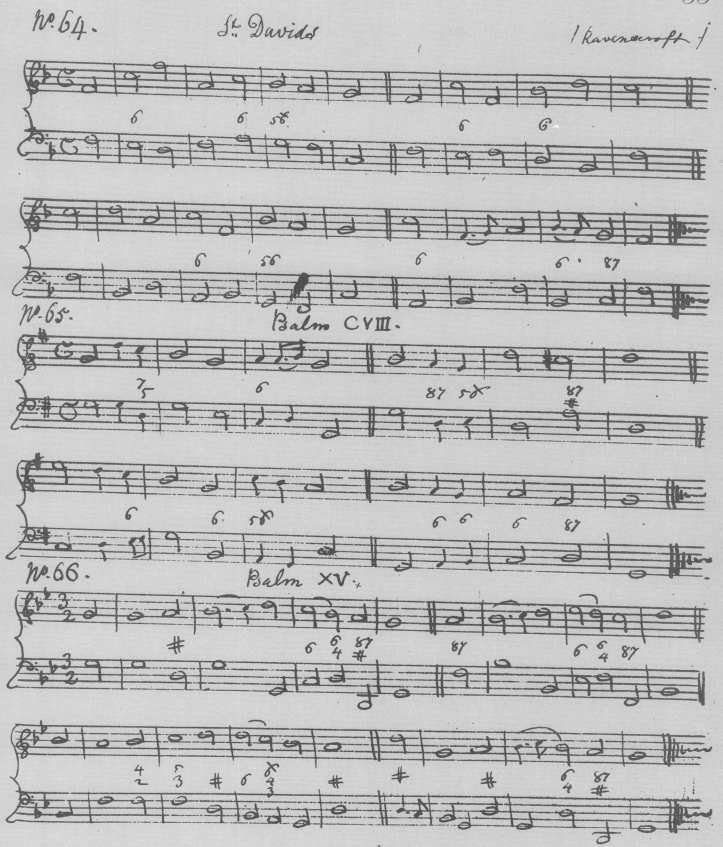

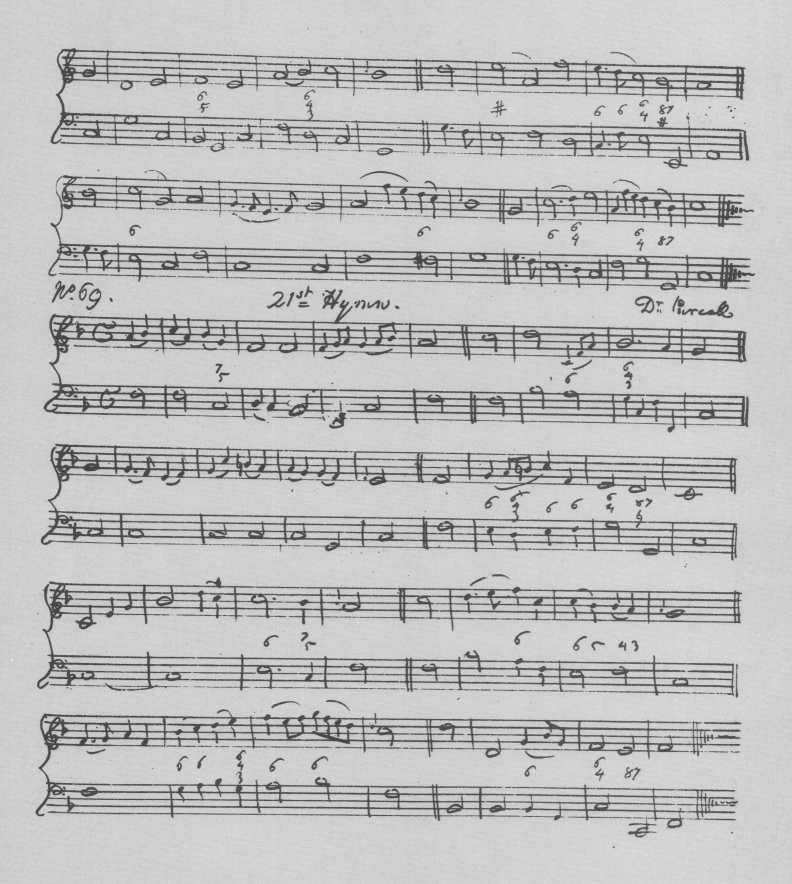

Nº 69.   21st Hymn.   Dr Purcell

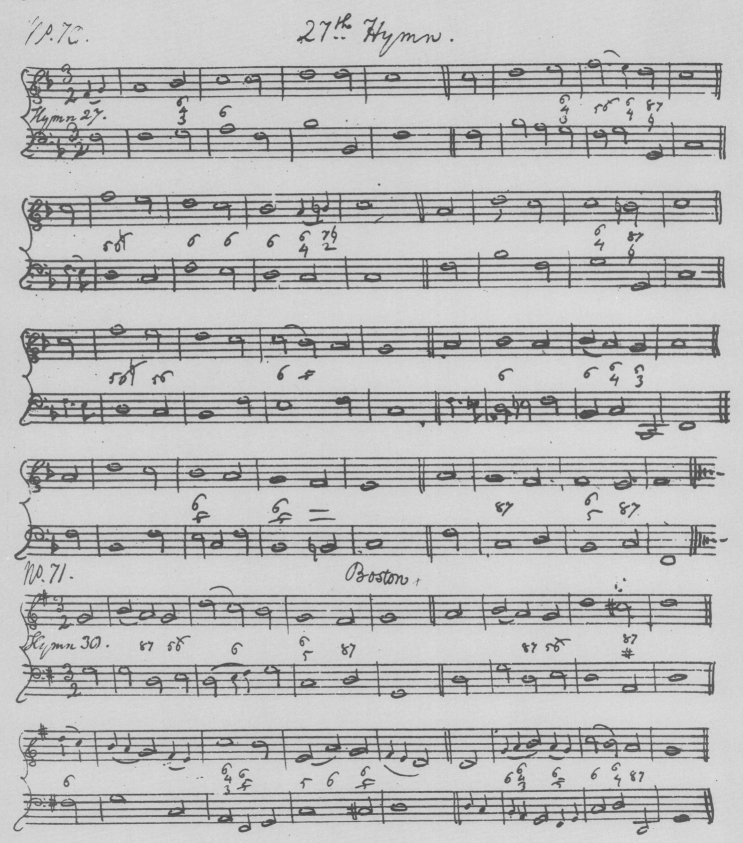

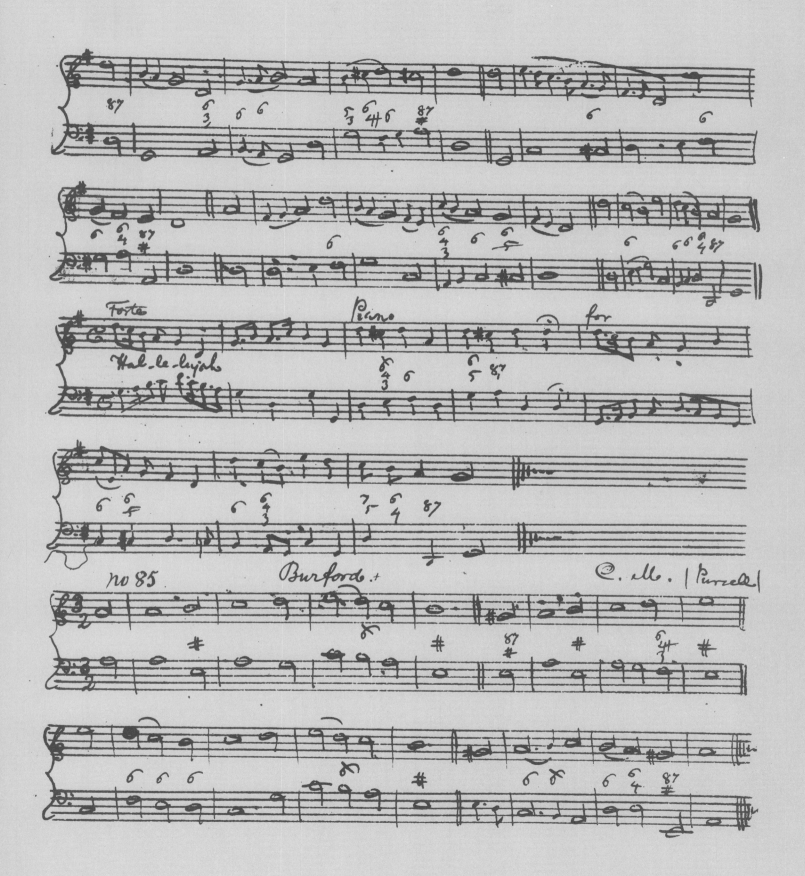

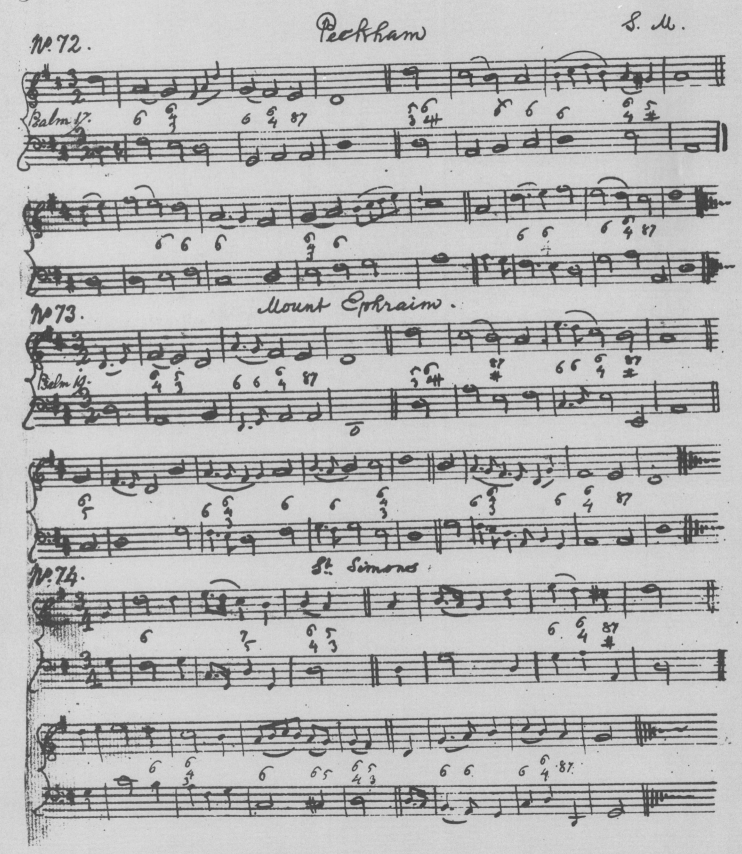

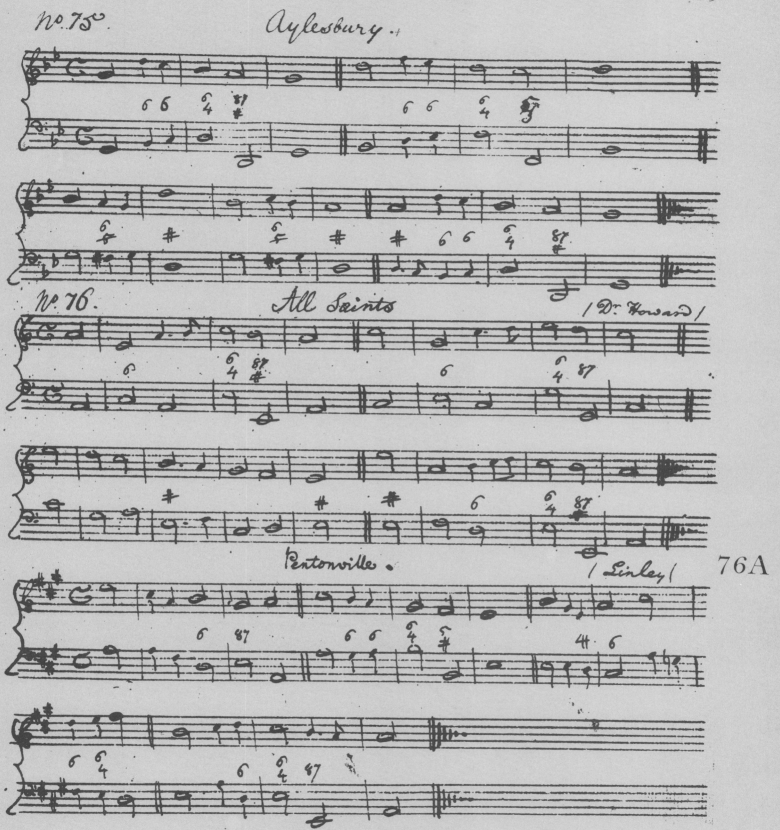

No. 77.

New Court..

Psalm 24.

No. 78.

St. Marks..

[Walton]

Psalm 16..

No. 79.

Lenox.

No. 80.

Ye boundless Realms of joy, Ex—alt your Makers fame His praise your

Song employ, A — bove the starry Frame. Your Voices raise ye

Cheru — bim and Se — ra — phim To sing his praise.

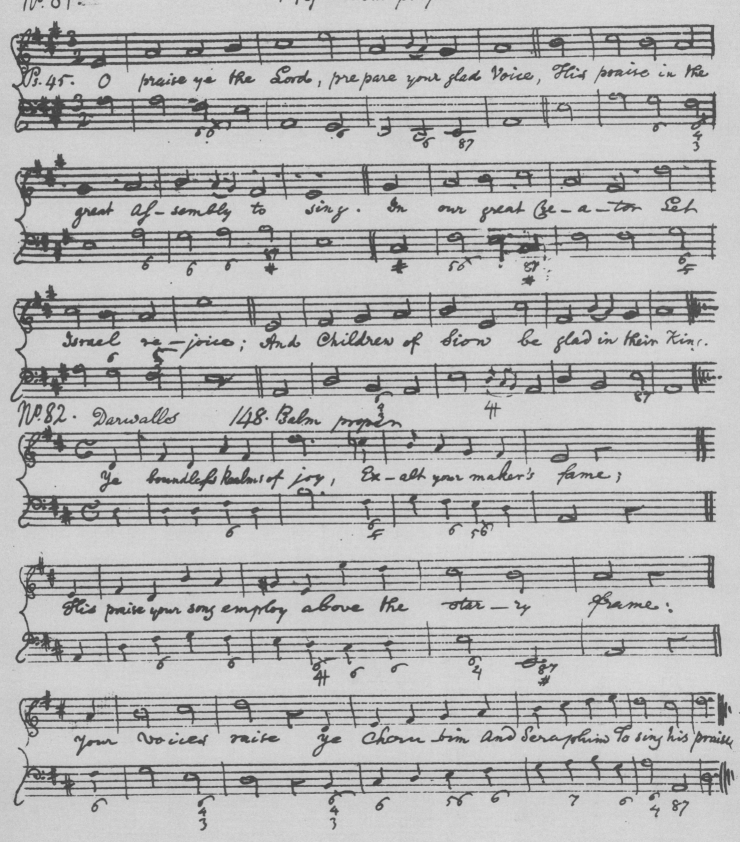

No. 81.   149. Balm proper.   Handel

Ps. 45.   O praise ye the Lord, prepare your glad Voice, His praise in the

great Af—sembly to   sing.   In   our great Cre—a—tor Let

Israel re—joice; And Children of Sion   be glad in their King.

No. 82. Darwalls   148. Balm proper

Ye boundless Realms of joy,   Ex—alt your maker's fame;

His praise your song employ above the   star—ry   Frame:

your voices raise   ye Cherubim And Seraphim To sing his praise

No. 83.　　　　　　Kent.　　　　　L. M.　　　[George Green]

No. 84.　　　28th Psalm Madan's　　　　　　　　　L. M.

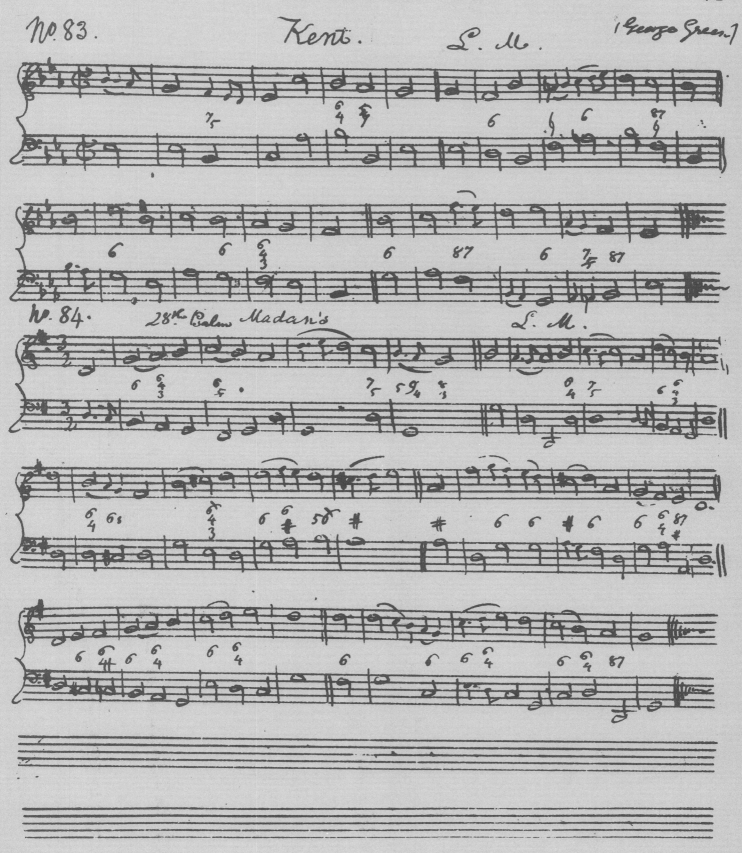

44

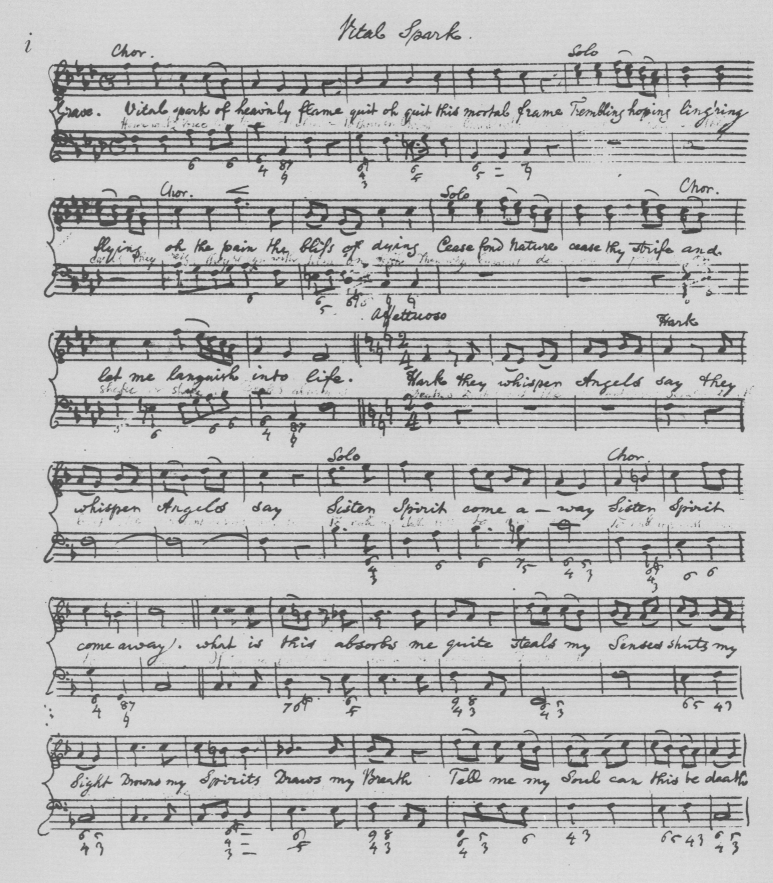

Vital Spark.

ii   Hymn for Easter

Chorus

Jesus Christ is ris'n to day, Hal......le-lu-jah our triumphant Holy Day

Hal....le-lu-jah.   Who did once up-on the Cross

Hal....le-lu-jah Suffer to re-deem our loss Hal......le-

lu-jah.   Hymns of praise then let us sing, unto Christ our

heavinly King Who endur'd the Cross & Grave, Sinners to re-deem and save

Hal-le-lujah Hal-le-lujah Halle-lujah, Hallelujah.

Volti

48

h Chaunt..

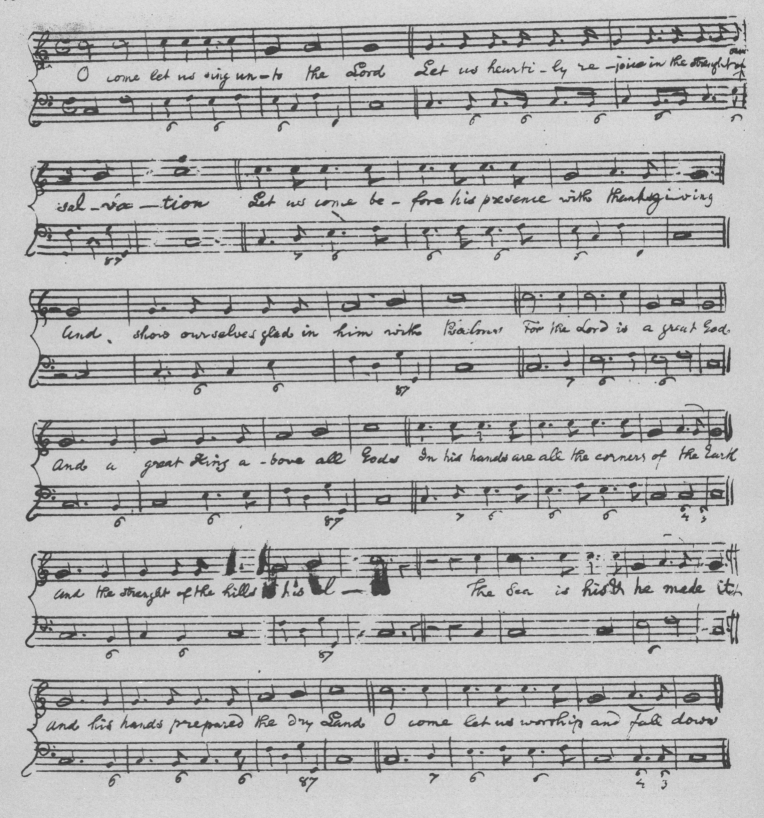

O come let us sing un—to the Lord. Let us hearti—ly re—joice in the strength of

isal—va——tion. Let us come be—fore his presence with thanksgiving

And. show ourselves glad in him with Psalmes. For the Lord is a great God.

And a great King a—bove all Gods. In his hands are all the corners of the Earth

And the strenght of the hills is his. The Sea is his & he made it.

And his hands prepared the dry Land. O come let us worship and fall down

52

k

Chaunt. double.

86

Vanhall's German Hymn.

54

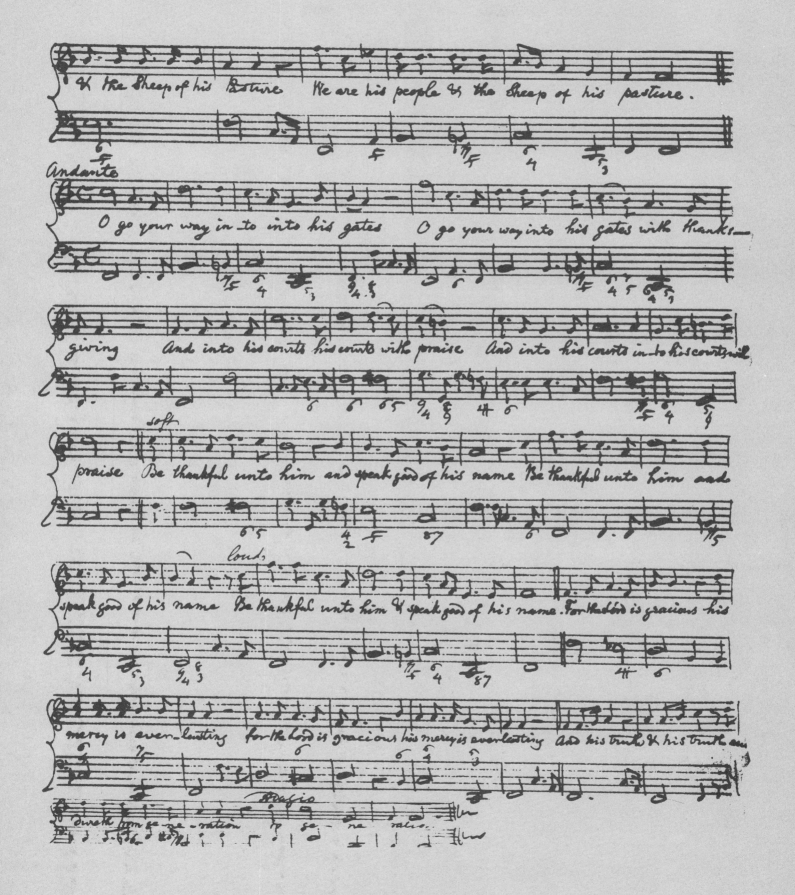

m

Deus misereatur.

God be merciful unto us, and bless us; And show us the light

of his countenance, and be merciful unto us. That thy way may be known

upon earth, Thy saving health among all Nations. Let the people praise thee,

O God; Yea, let all the people praise thee. O let the Nations rejoice & be

glad; for thou shalt judge the folk righteously, and govern the nations upon Earth.

Let the people praise thee, O God; yea, let all the people praise thee.

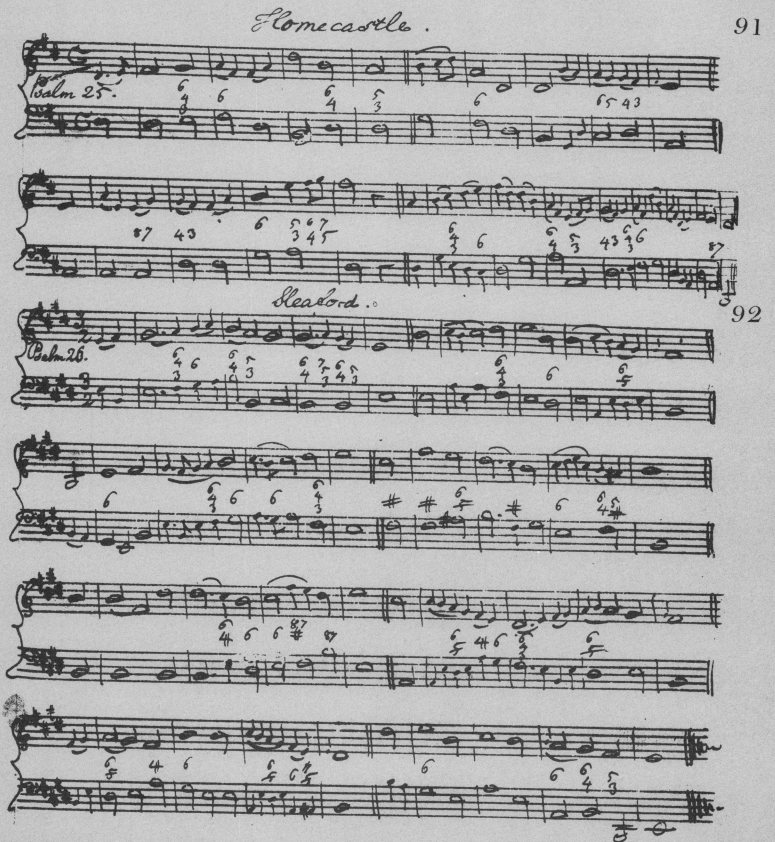

Homecastle.

91

Psalm 25.

Sleaford.

92

Psalm 26.

St Luke's.

93 Psalm 32.

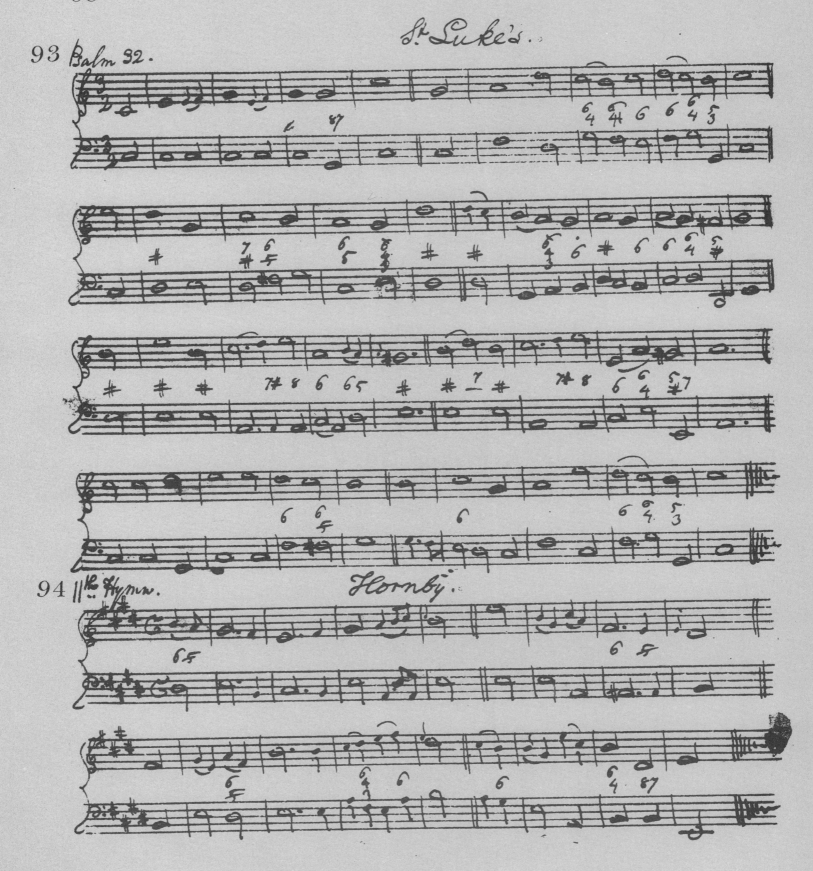

94 11th Hymn.   Hornby.

Whittelsea

Lincoln.

61

95

96

62

97 13th Hymn.

98 32th Hymn.

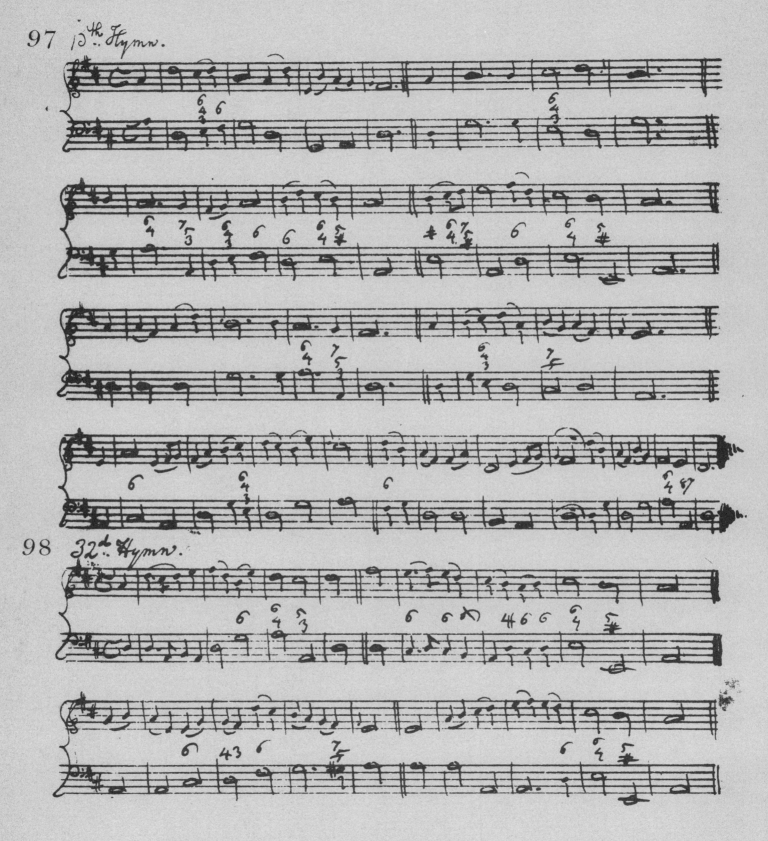

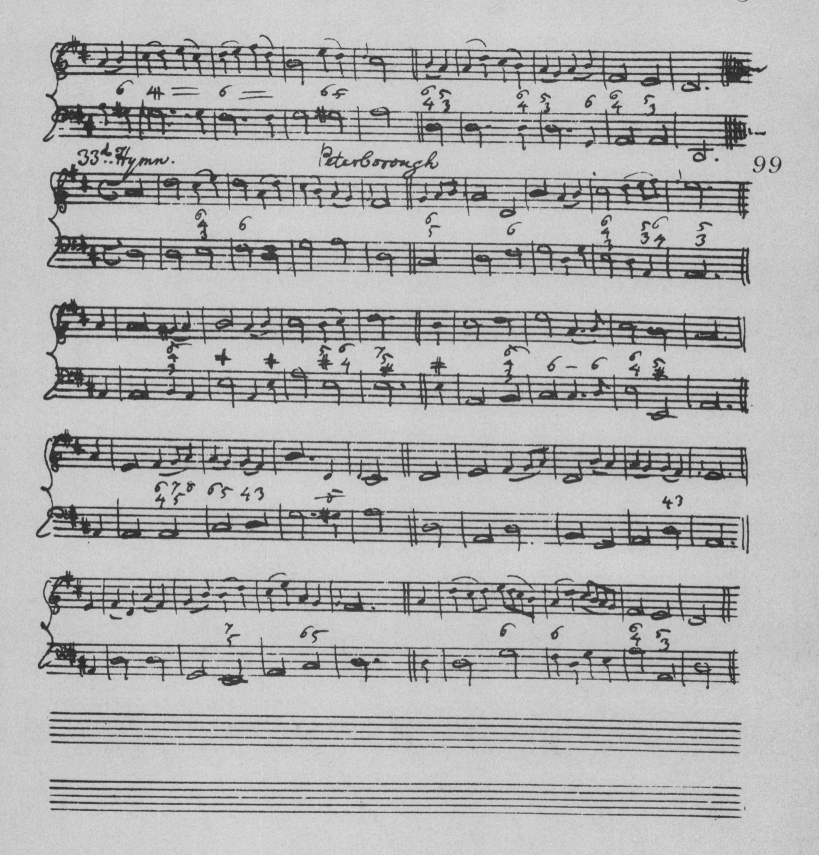

33th Hymn.   Peterborough   99

Evening Hymn.

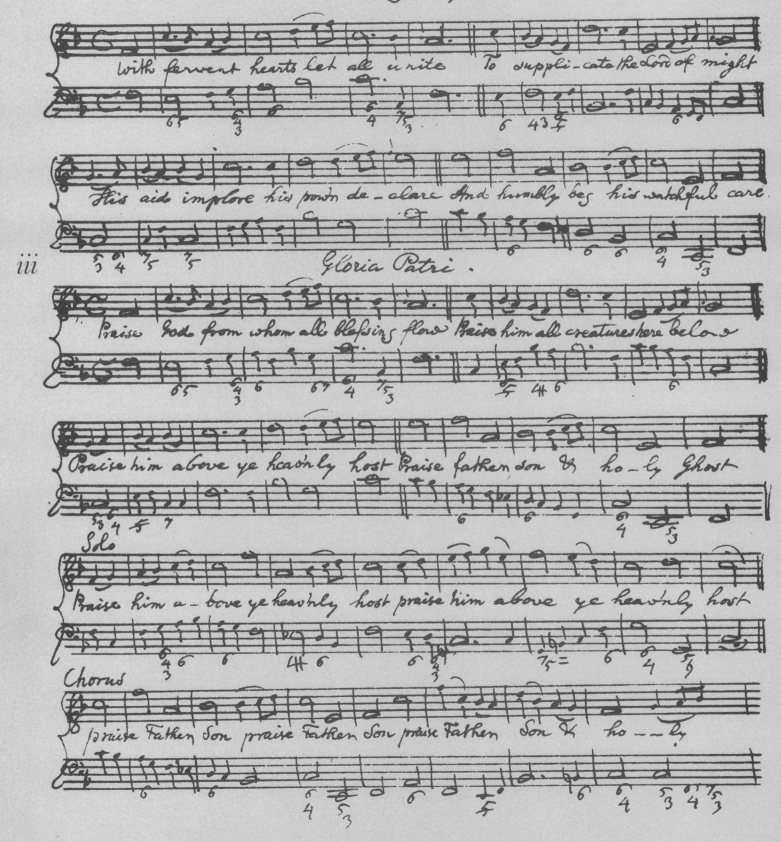

With fervent hearts let all unite   To suppli-cate the Lord of might

His aid implore his powr de-clare And humbly beg his watchful care.

Gloria Patri.

Praise God from whom all blessing flow Praise him all creatures here below

Praise him above ye heavnly host Praise father son & ho—ly Ghost

Solo

Praise him a-bove ye heavnly host praise him above ye heavnly host

Chorus

O praise Father son praise Father son praise Father Son & ho——ly

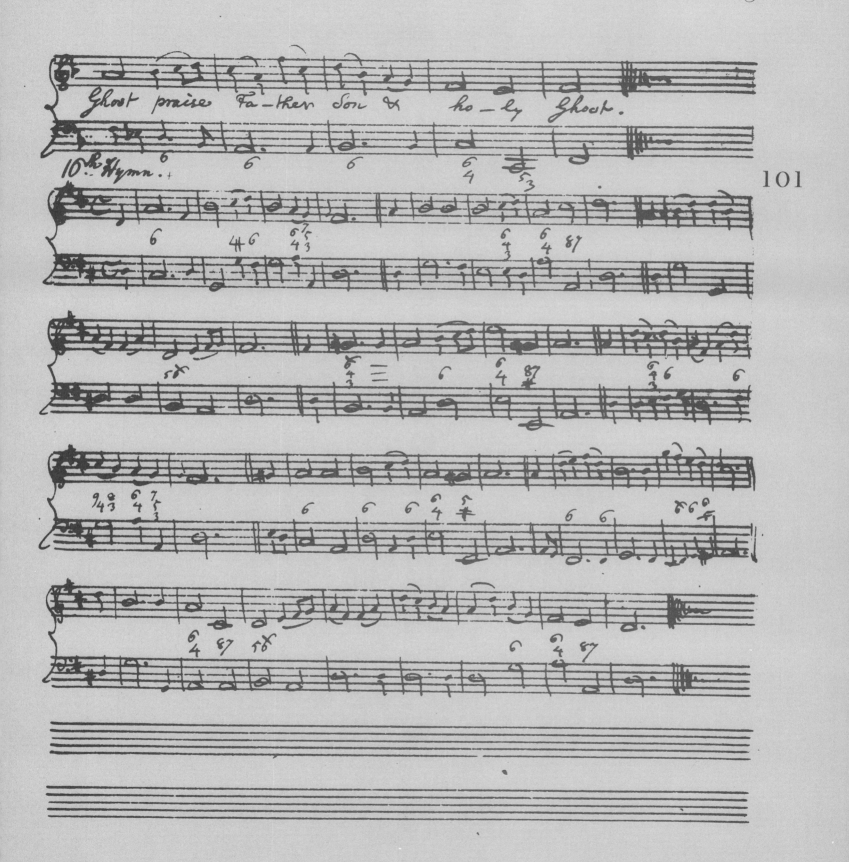

Ghost praise Fa—ther Son & ho—ly Ghost.

10th Hymn.+

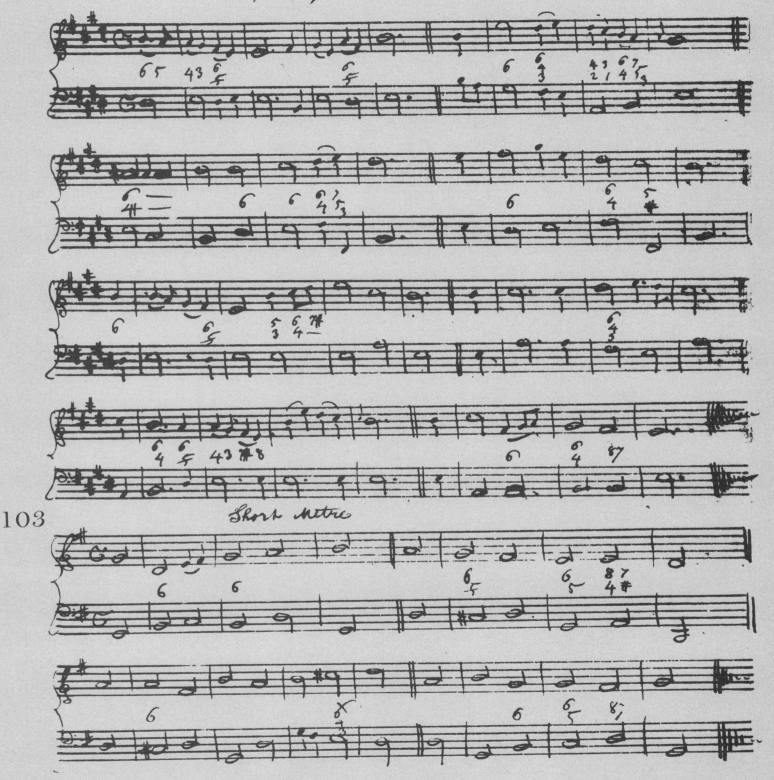

29th Hymn.

Short Metre

Christmas Day.

New years Day.

Chaunt +

Ghost be with us all a—ven more A—men.

104   *Hymn 29th.*   T. Welsh

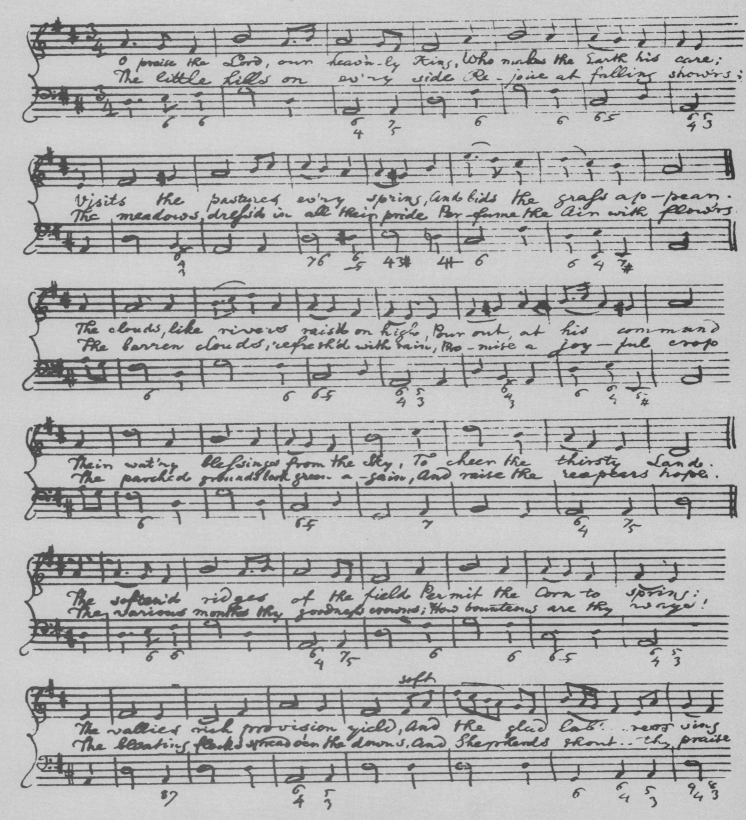

O praise the Lord, our heav'nly King, Who makes the Earth his care;
The little hills on ev'ry side Re-joice at falling show'rs;

Visits the pastures ev'ry spring, And bids the grass appear.
The meadows, dress'd in all their pride Per-fume the Air with flow'rs.

The clouds, like rivers rais'd on high, Pour out, at his command
The barren clouds, refresh'd with rain, Pro-mise a joy-ful crop

Their wat'ring blessings from the sky, To cheer the thirsty Lands.
The parched ground looks green a-gain, And raise the reapers hope.

The soften'd ridges of the field Permit the Corn to spring;
The various months thy goodness crowns; How bounteous are thy ways!

The valleys rich provision yield, And the glad lab'rers sing;
The bleating flocks spread o'er the downs, And Shepherds shout thy praise.

70

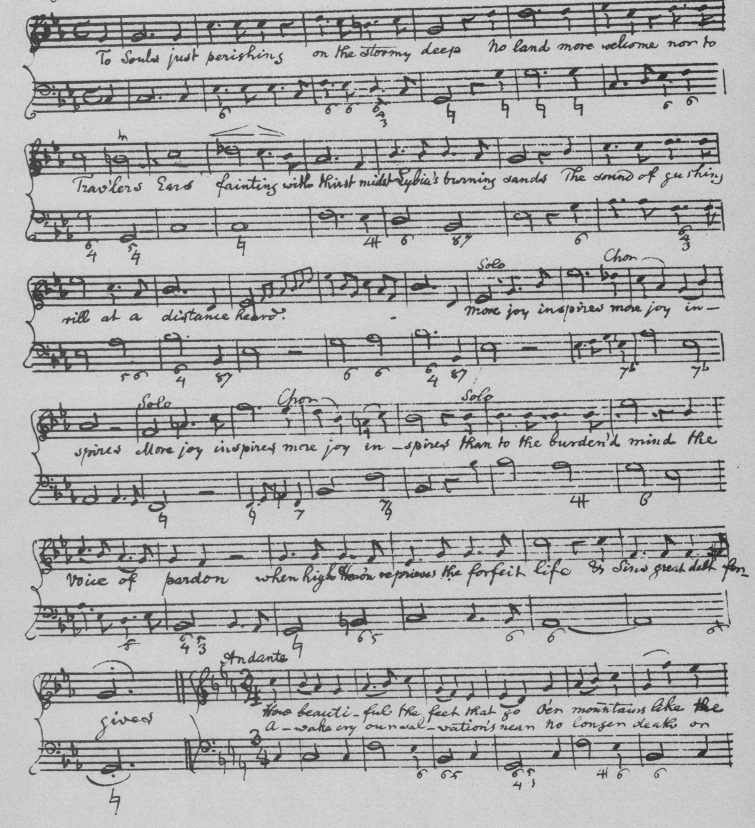

Hymn for Easter.

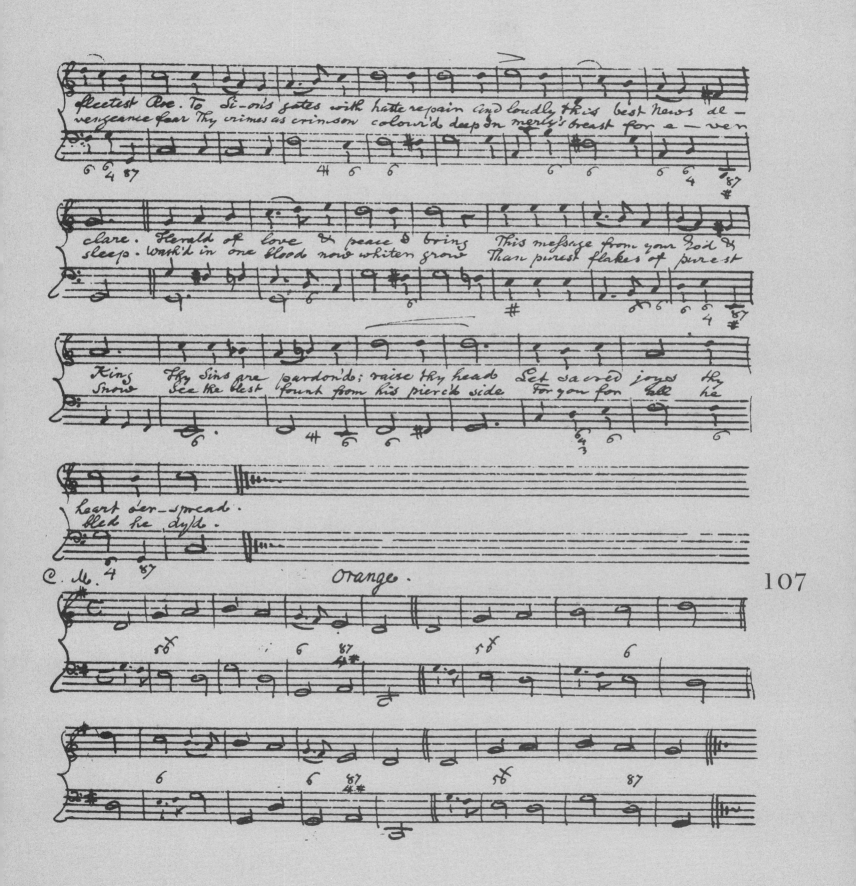

Gloria in Excelsis

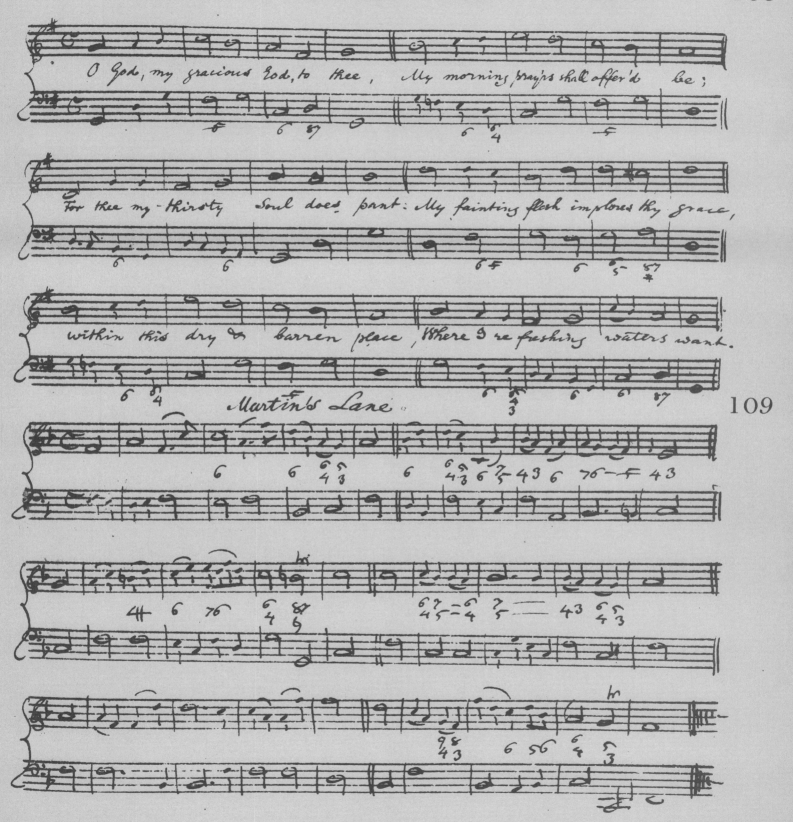

Psalm 5. the same Metre as New Court

O God, my gracious God, to thee, My morning prayrs shall offer'd be;

For thee my thirsty Soul does pant: My fainting flesh implores thy grace,

within this dry & barren place, Where I refreshing waters want.

Martin's Lane

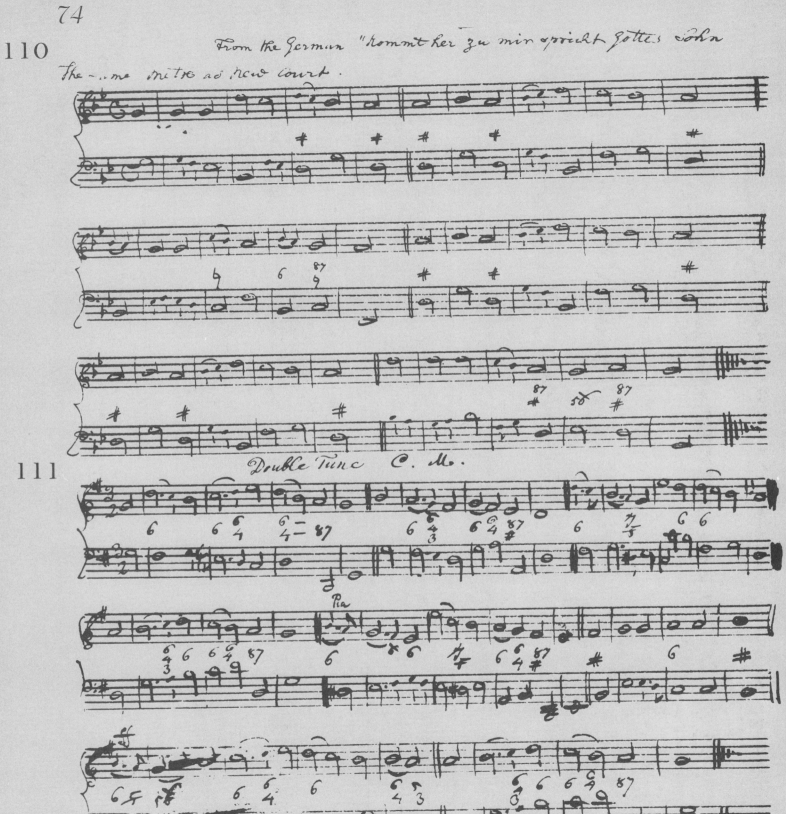

76

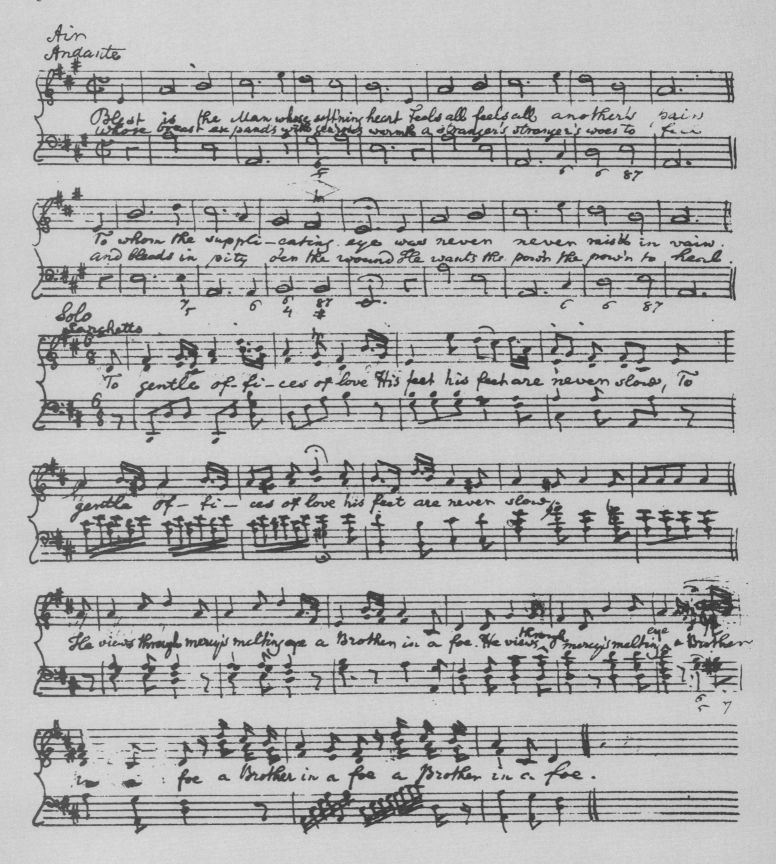

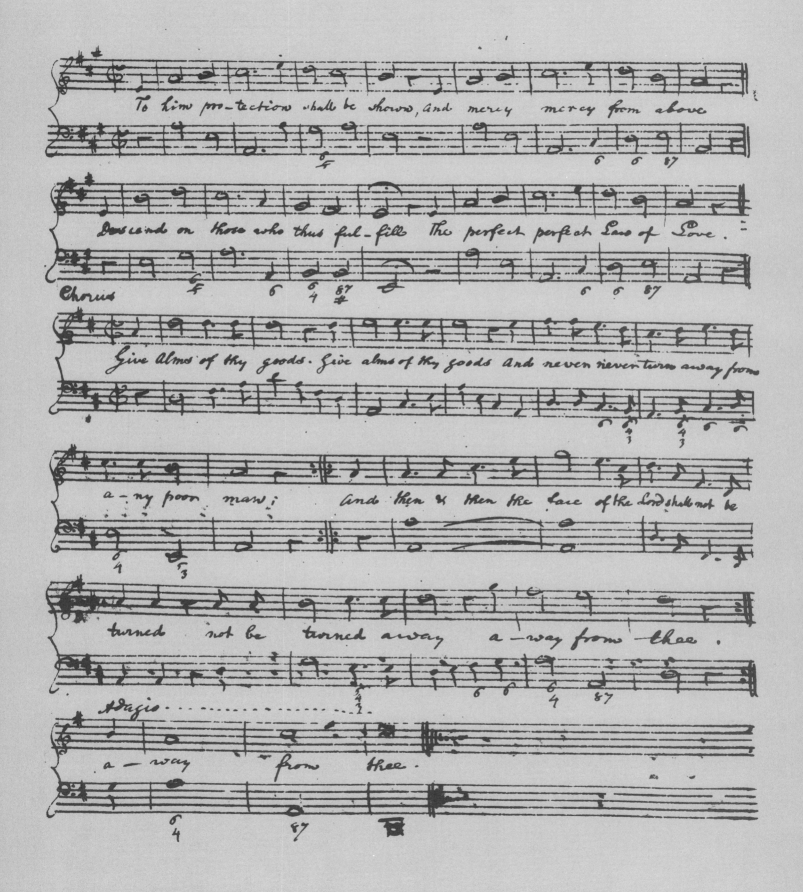

II

Anthem

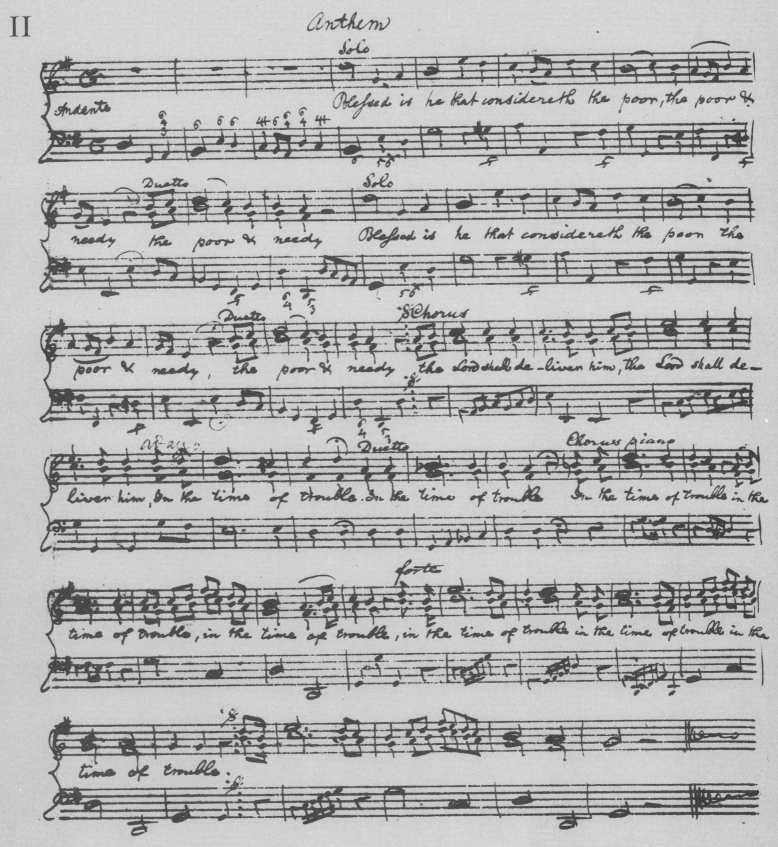

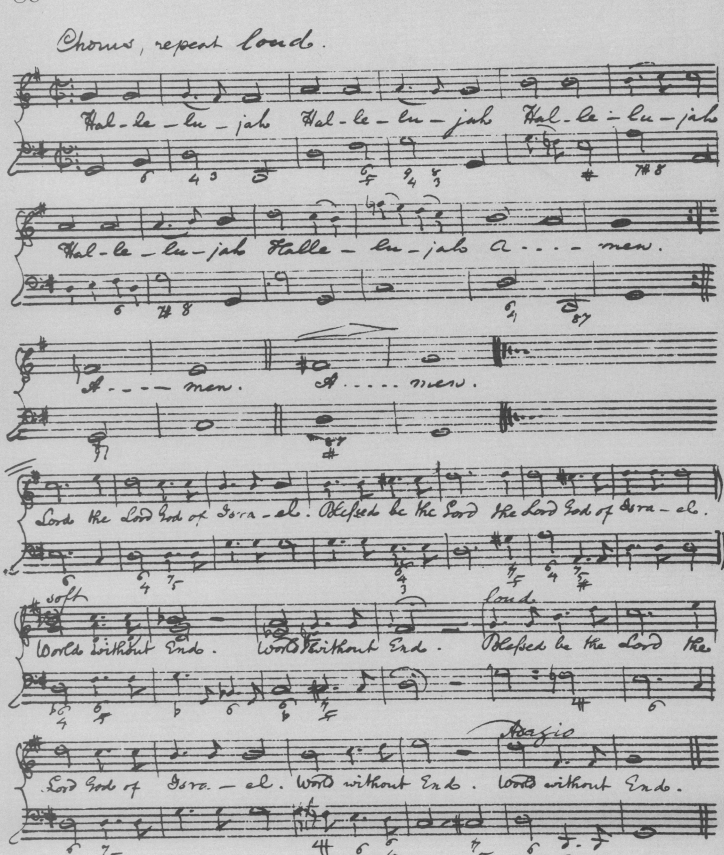

Christmas Hymn.

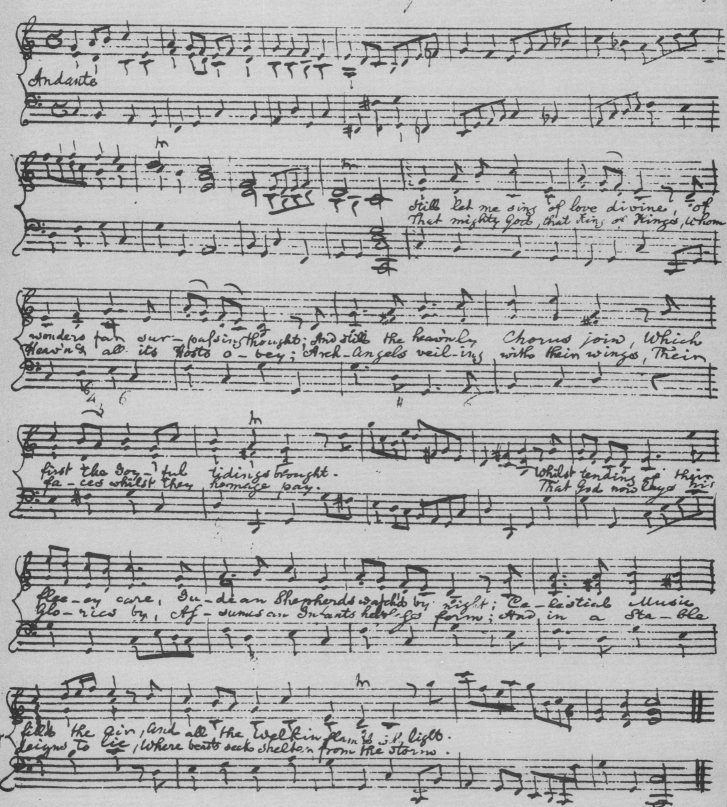

Andante

Still let me sing of love divine, of
That mighty God, that King of Kings, whom

wonders far sur-passing thought; And still the heav'nly Chorus join, which
Heav'n's all its hosts o-bey; Arch-Angels veil-ing with their wings, their

first the joy-ful tidings brought.
fa-ces whilst they homage pay.

Whilst tending their
That God now lays his

flee-cy care, Ju-de-an Shepherds watch'd by night; Ce-lestial Music
Glo-ries by, Assumes an Infants helpless form; And in a Sta-ble

fills the air, And all the Welkin flam'd with light.
deigns to lie, Where beasts seek shelter from the storm.

Duett

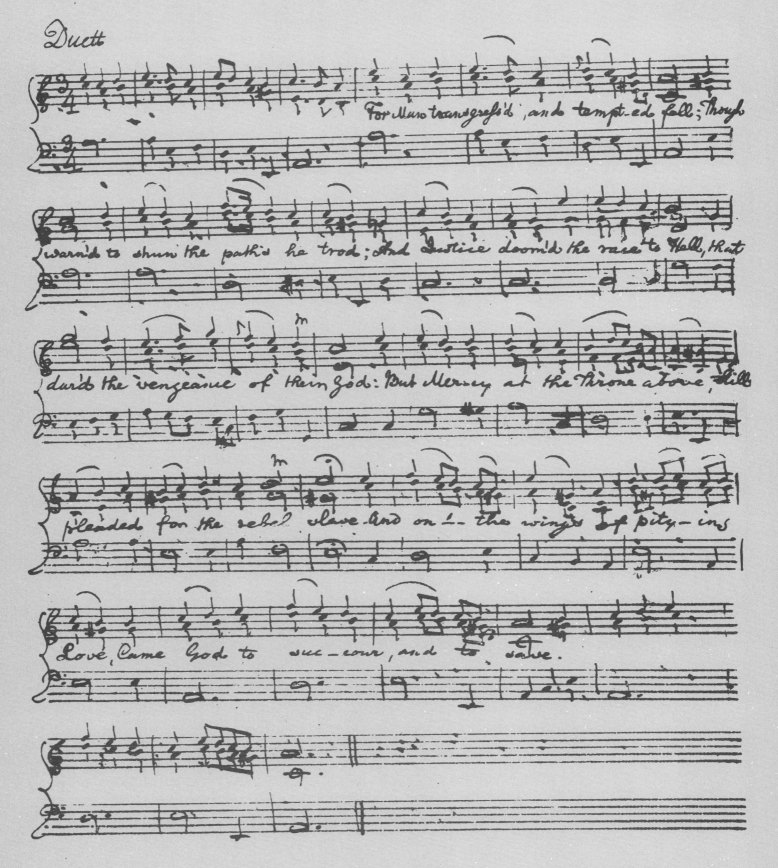

For Man transgress'd, and tempted fell; Though warn'd to shun the paths he trod; And Justice doom'd the race to Hell, that dar'd the vengeance of their God: But Mercy at the Throne above, still pleaded for the rebel slave And on the wings of pity-ing Love, came God to suc-cour, and to save.

Anthem for Christmas = Day.

[C. Bond]

IV

86

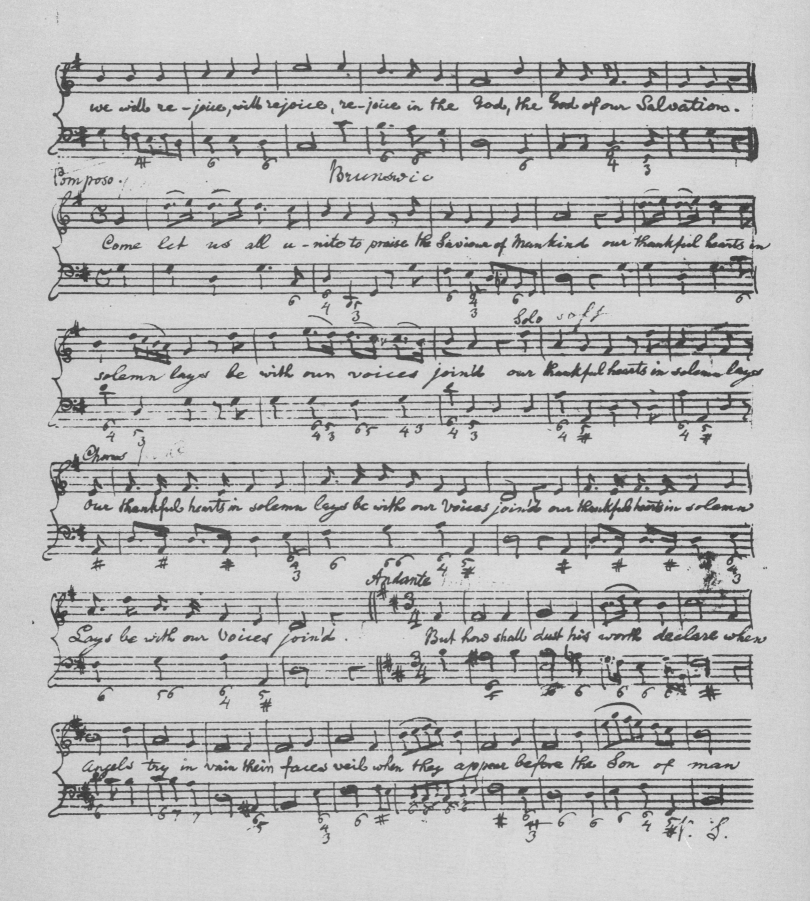

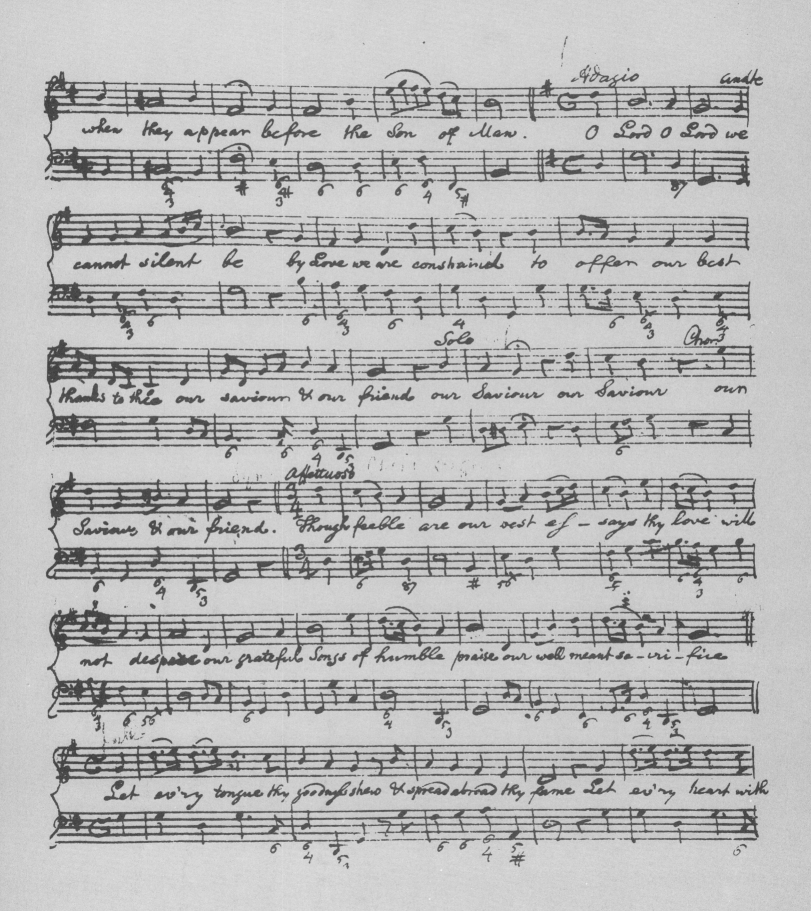

88

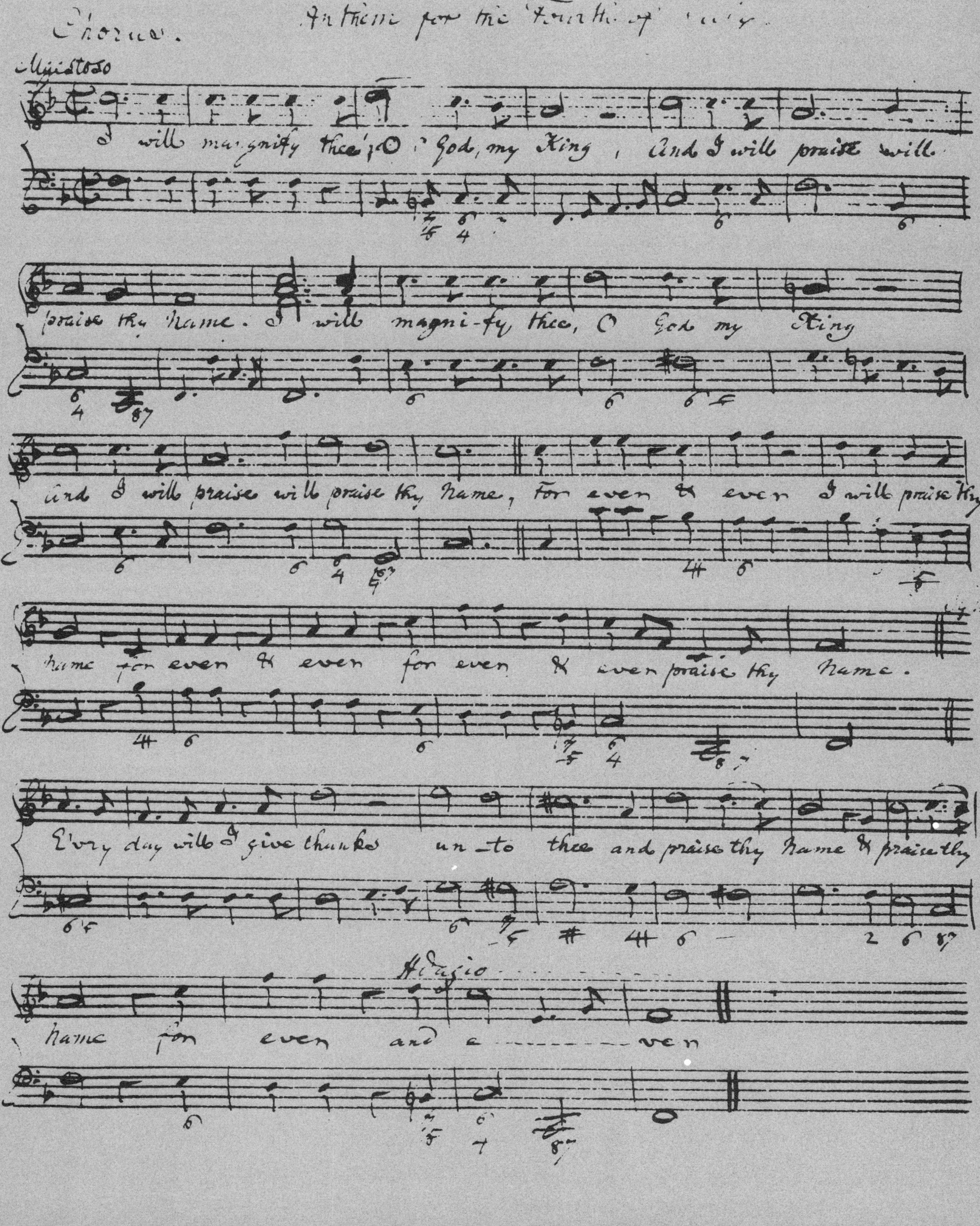
Chorus.
I will magnify thee, O God, my King, And I will praise will praise thy Name. I will magni-fy thee, O God my King
And I will praise will praise thy Name, for ever & ever I will praise thy Name for ever & ever for ever & ever praise thy Name.
Ev'ry day will I give thanks un-to thee and praise thy Name & praise thy Name for ever and e-ven
Adagio

90

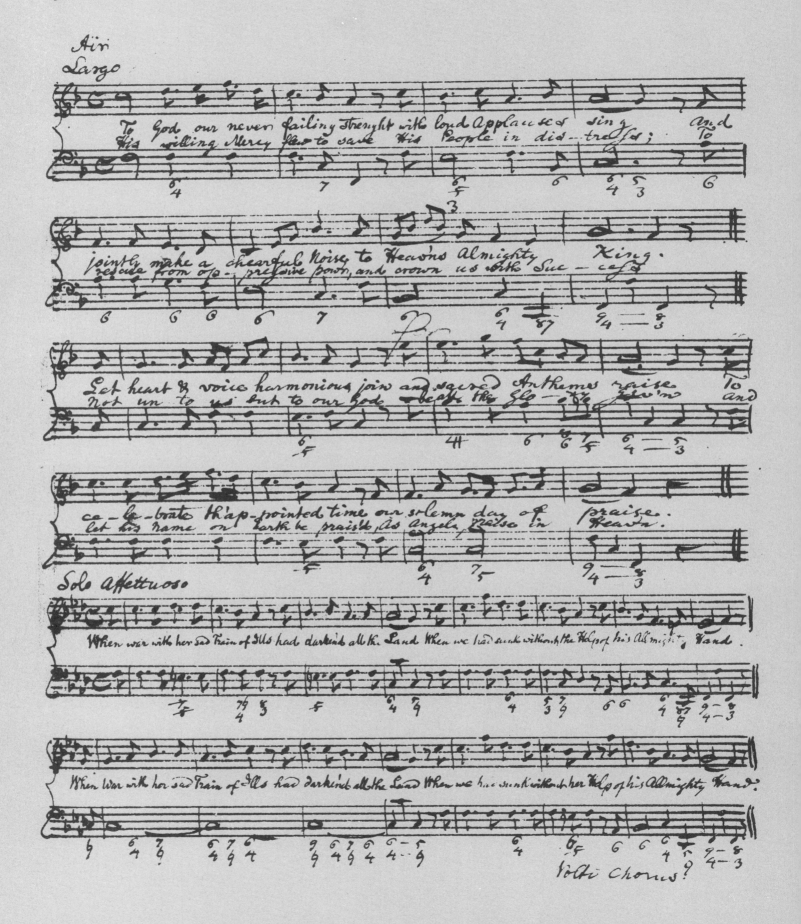

Chorus

Notes to the Facsimile

The facsimile of Jacob Eckhard's manuscript choirmaster's book has been prepared from the one copy known to be in existence.[1] This copy is signed "Jacob Eckhard, Sen.," and dated 1809 on the cover. It is evidently the organist's copy, for it bears on the first page a copy of the vestry's "Duties of the Organist agreed to February 27, 1803." Also, scattered throughout are penciled notes of registration for the organ at St. Michael's. The manuscript descended to Eckhard's granddaughter, Priscilla Perkins, of Camden, S. C., who gave it to Thomas P. O'Neale, then a young man and later a well-known musician of Charleston. After O'Neale's death, his widow presented it to St. Michael's Church in 1916.

The fascimile differs from the original only in the arrangement of the five anthems at the end of the collection. These anthems were copied into the manuscript beginning at the rear of the volume and working forward with the book turned upside down. In consequence, the last page of Anthem [V] faces upside down the last page containing tunes. The present facsimile concludes with the anthems numbered according to their original sequence but rearranged from front to back in numerical order and turned right-side up for ease of reading. Consequently, the first page of Anthem [I] now faces the last page containing tunes.

Signature and Date. Eckhard's signature on the front cover is consistent with the single hand of the manuscript throughout. The same hand has supplied marginal notes in the copy of the *Choral-Book* (1816) in the Charleston Library Society.

The date records Eckhard's appointment as organist. It is without doubt also the date of the preparation of all or most of the manuscript. There are indications, however, that the unnumbered tunes [86–111] and the chants interspersed among them may derive from a secondary and presumably later stage of compilation. The fact that these tunes are unnumbered distinguishes them immediately, but their distinctness is further confirmed by their arrangement. Tunes 1–85 are arranged on the basis of meter with no regard to the sequence of numbered psalms and hymns in the *Selection;* tunes [86–111] are arranged generally according to the numbered psalms and hymns in the *Selection* with no regard to their meters (tunes 94, 95, and 96 are out of order probably because of the size of the page). It is possible to see a third stage of compilation in tunes

---

[1] This copy is in the Manuscript Collection of St. Michael's Church, deposited in the Library of the South Carolina Historical Society. The facsimile has been reproduced from microfilm made and processed in the photographic laboratories of the Department of Art, Duke University. This edition has been manufactured to conform to the dimensions of the original.

[101–111] which follow neither pattern, but the evidence is too slight to be convincing. Furthermore, a diligent search in the tune books of the eighteenth and nineteenth centuries has failed to reveal prior examples of most of these unnumbered tunes. It is unlikely that these tunes, mostly with English place-names, were composed by Eckhard; it is rather more probable that they derive from one or two tune books as yet undetected and possibly dating after 1809.

With two exceptions [93, 99] the unnumbered tunes are set to psalms and hymns without settings in the series of tunes 1–85; they are thus complementary to these tunes. The hand of the manuscript appears to show neither ageing nor differing characteristics. If there were two stages of compilation, it is unlikely that they were separated by a long interval. Eckhard's collection is the earliest manuscript surviving in America consisting of music for the Episcopal church.

The Notice. That this *Notice* is printed strongly suggests that Eckhard prepared other "Manuscript Books" of which no examples are extant, for he would hardly have had such a label printed unless he had needed multiple copies of it. It does not necessarily follow, of course, that the other "Manuscript Books" were in every respect uniform with the organist's collection. It could well be that the books used by the "Members of the Choir" were much smaller; perhaps they contained melodies only or fewer tunes. They may have resembled the published *Choral-Book* (1816) more closely than the full collection of 1809.

Duties of the Organist. These are copied from the Minutes of the Vestry of St. Michael's Church; they are reprinted in G. W. Williams, *St. Michael's* (Columbia, 1951), pp. 208–9.

The Tunes, Hymns, Chants, and Anthems. Each tune, hymn, chant, or anthem is noted below, numbers being provided in brackets for those lacking them. The notes include, after the name of the tune,

the composer if given by Eckhard or some comment on the source (where identified). Then follows where appropriate the notation: in 1785 (the hymnal proposed by the General Convention of 1785, published in 1786), or 1816 (Eckhard's *Choral-Book*), or 1940 (*The Hymnal 1940* of the Protestant Episcopal Church). Then follows the text for which the tune was used. The psalm numbers in Arabic figures refer to the psalm numbers in the *Selection* (Charleston, 1792); in parentheses in small Roman numerals follow the scriptural numbers (Psalms of David) in the *New Version* of metrical psalms (*NV*) of Tate and Brady (1696) and, where appropriate, the notation that only selected verses have been used (sel. vv.). The hymn number refers to the *Selection* of 1792 with the source, where known. Finally, abbreviated references to the List of Works Consulted follow in parentheses; these are keyed to the sigla given in Section A of the list. Texts and titles are presented in modern spellings and standard forms.

In preparing the following notes, the present editor has been guided by the desire to annotate not the tunes but the book. In consequence, the tunes are not invariably traced to their origins, as they are—and properly—in the various companions and handbooks consulted; the aim has been to discover rather where Eckhard might have found the tunes he copied. It has become evident, in examining the various collections of tunes, that Eckhard's collection does not depend on any single volume or on any few volumes. It shows, rather, a very extensive knowledge of psalmody and hymnody of the eighteenth and early nineteenth centuries. With the exceptions of the proposed hymnal of 1785 and Pilsbury's *United States' Sacred Harmony,* no volume has been specifically identified as having served Eckhard as a "copy-text," and indeed no single volume could have provided all or even a large part of the tunes, chants, hymns, or anthems in this collection.

The present editor is conscious of his inadequacies in failing to identify some of the tunes and chants, and he invites his learned readers to inform him of identifications that they can make.

Key to Numbering System

Psalm and Hymn Tunes: Numbers 1–111.
Chants: Numbers a–u.
Hymns in Special Settings: Numbers i–iv.
Anthems: Numbers I–V.

[No. 0.1.] PORTUGAL. Appears in Pilsbury, *U. S. Sacred Harmony* (1799), somewhat simpler version in Eckhard. It is attributed to Thorley. In 1816.

Portugal and *Wells*, [0.2], are placed without number on the flyleaf of the manuscript and without ascription of text. They are both Long Meter and may have accompanied a doxology or *Gloria Patri* as tunes in weekly use.

[No. 0.2.] WELLS. In *American Harmony* (1793) where it is attributed to Aaron Williams. Dr. Sander suggests Israel Holdroyd for the composer. Eckhard's barring differs from the original. See [0.1].

No. 1. ST. PETER's. Valton. In 1816. For Psalm 46 (*NV*, cl).

No. 2. ST. PHILIP's. Valton. The final cadences contain three-part harmony. For Psalm 12 (*NV*, xxxii, sel. vv.).

No. 3. ST. JOHN's NEW. Valton. For Psalm 6 (*NV*, xviii, sel. vv.).

No. 4. ST. MICHAEL's. Valton. This minor tune, named for St. Michael's Church, appears also twice in the Charleston Museum Copy-book where it is attributed to Valton and set to the 137th Psalm. In 1816. For Psalm 39 (*NV*, cxxxvii, sel. vv.).

No. 5. ST. ANN's NEW. Valton. Contains unusually rich harmonic structure. In 1816. For Hymn 26 (author not identified).

No. 6. ANGEL's HYMN. An eighteenth-century version of Orlando Gibbons' *Song 34*, published first in 1623. In 1785, 1816, 1940. Eckhard's version has several passing notes not in 1785. For Psalm 31 (*NV*, ciii, sel. vv.). (Satcher.)

No. 7. CHARLESTON. Source not identified; possibly Eckhard. In 1816. For Psalm 18 (*NV*, lvii, sel. vv.).

No. 8. ISLINGTON. This tune is included in *American Harmony* (1769) where it is set to Psalm 117 and attributed to A. W. (Aaron Williams). In 1816. For Psalm 22 (*NV*, lxxxviii, sel. vv.).

No. 9. OLD HUNDRED PSALM. Composed by Louis Bourgeois for the *Genevan Psalter* of 1551. "The only tune which has been preserved intact throughout the entire history of metrical psalmody and modern hymnody, and as such deservedly ranks at the head of all Protestant church music" (*Comp.*, p. 183). In 1785, 1816, 1940. In 1816, Eckhard claims its descent from "Herr Gott dich loben alle wir." Also in Charleston Museum Copy-book and Pilsbury, *U. S. Sacred Harmony* (1799), in both of which it is attributed to Martin Luther. For Psalm 30 (*NV*, c).

No. 10. LUTHER's HYMN. In spite of the name, Dr. Sander has observed, there is no evidence that the tune was written by Luther. It first appeared anonymously in Joseph Klug's *Geistliche Lieder* (Wittenberg, 1535) and has in variant forms been traditionally set to Luther's text, "Nun freut euch, lieber Christen gemein," according to Dr. Ellinwood. In 1816. Eckhard there ascribes it to "Es ist gewisslich an der Zeit." Zahn 4429a. The text provided (also in 1816) is the first stanza of Hymn 33, by Philip Doddridge (*Hymns*, 1755).

No. 11. ST. MICHAEL's NEW. Rev. Dr. Purcell. This tune is typical of the florid tunes of the latter part of the eighteenth century. For Hymn 20, by Philip Doddridge (*Hymns*, 1755).

No. 12. PORTUGUESE HYMN. This tune was first printed in *An Essay on the Plain Church Chant* (1782). Dr. Sander notes that it received its name from being first heard in London in the Portuguese Chapel by the Duke of Leeds. Opinions as to the composer differ. In 1816, 1940. The fuguing characteristics are not retained, and modern singers will hardly recognize the familiar tune *Adeste fideles* ("O come, all ye faithful"). For Hymn 34, by

Philip Doddridge (*Hymns,* 1755). (*Comp.; Handbook.*) (In 1816, the tune is set to the first stanza of Hymn 34.)

No. 13. CAMDEN. Though bearing a local name, *Camden* is actually the chorale "Mach's mit mir, Gott, nach deiner Gut" (Chorale 124, *Bach Gesellschaft,* xxxix, 242). It was composed by Johann Hermann Schein in 1607 and published in 1628. Zahn 2383. In 1816, where it is called "Hymn 90," the number referring to the *Evangelical Lutheran Hymn Book.*

No. 14. TRADD STREET. This locally named tune is the chorale "Herr Jesu Christ dich zu uns wend," from *Pensum Sacrum* (1648). Zahn 624. In 1816.

No. 15. ST. DENNIS's. Source not identified. In 1816. Also in *A Selection of Psalm Tunes for the Use of the Protestant Episcopal Church in . . . New York* (New York, 1812).

No. 16. PLEYEL'S HYMN. This tune was made available for church use in Arnold and Callcott's *Psalms of David for the Use of Parish Churches* (1791) from Ignaz Pleyel's String Quartet, op. 7, no. 4 (1782) where it is the theme of a set of variations. In 1940. (*Comp.*)

No. 17. ST. MICHAEL'S NEWEST. One of the many cognate tunes of *Winchester New.* Possibly from "Wer nur den lieben Gott lässt walten" in *Musikalisches Hand-Buch* (Hamburg, 1690), Zahn 2781 (introduced into the English tradition in *Foundery Tune Book* (1742) or from *Crasselius* in *Geistreiches Gesangbuch* (Halle, 1704), Zahn 3067, itself an extension of Zahn 2781. In 1940. See also [105].

No. 18. ST. PHILIP'S NEW. This locally named tune is the chorale "Wenn wir in höchsten Nöten sein," which appeared first in the *Genevan Psalter* of 1543. It is the chorale theme of Bach's Cantata 179 (*Bach Gesellschaft,* xxxix, 272).

No. 19. BRAMCOATE. Appeared also in Pilsbury, *U. S. Sacred Harmony* (1799). In 1816.

No. 20. HACKNEY. J. H. Stevens. For Psalm 32 (*NV,* cvi, sel. vv.).

No. 21. WELLS's ROW. This tune, concluding with sixfold hallelujahs, appeared in Rippon's *Selection* (1791). It is also in Pilsbury, *U. S. Sacred Harmony* (1799). In 1816.

Nos. 22 and 23. MAGDALEN, First and Second Parts. [Valton.] These tunes appear together also in the Charleston Museum Copy-book where they are set to Psalm 139 and attributed to Valton. First Part in 1816. For Psalm 40 (*NV,* cxxxix, sel. vv.). The division of the psalm into two parts is evidently the work of Smith and Purcell.

No. 24. CHURCH STREET. J. H. Stevens. This tune is named for the street on which St. Philip's Church stands. It was revived at a service of special music at St. Michael's Church on February 10, 1952, when it was used for the text "How firm a foundation."

No. 25. HEREFORD. Rev. Dr. Purcell. This double tune is named for the composer's birthplace. It was revived at a service of special music at St. Michael's Church on February 10, 1952, when it was used for the text "How wondrous and great, Thy works, God of Light." For Psalm 23 (*NV,* lxxxix, sel. vv.).

No. 26. OXFORD. Rev. Dr. Purcell. This tune is named for the composer's university. For Psalm 27 (*NV,* xcvi, sel. vv.). Eckhard thought of this as a double tune, but it is more accurately described as two triplets and a couplet (see the stanza form), 888.888.88.

No. 27. PSALM 8TH. Mr. Cook. From the *Foundling Collection* (1774), where it is set to Psalm viii.

No. 28. DENBIGH. From Madan's *Lock Collection* (1769). In 1816. The text provided is Hymn 31, Joseph Addison's splendid paraphrase of Psalm xix, from *The Spectator,* No. 265 (August 23, 1712). In 1816.

No. 29. DARTFORD. In John Rippon's *Selection of Psalm and Hymn Tunes* (1791), no. 127. The text provided is Hymn 24 by Robert Seagrave (*Hymns,* 1742).

No. 30. DENMARK. From Madan's *Lock Collection* (1769). In 1816. The text provided is Hymn 36, Isaac Watts' paraphrase of Psalm c (*Psalms of David Imitated,* 1719), as altered by John Wesley (*A Collection* [Charleston,

1737]), and as further altered in Madan's *Collection*. An optional verse in two settings is added to the four in the Charleston *Selection* of 1792. That verse in a setting for duet appears also in the "anthem" in Pilsbury, *U. S. Sacred Harmony* (1799) and in 1816.

No. 31. LONDON NEW. Called *Newton* at its first publication in *The Psalms of David* (1635), the Scottish Psalter, this tune later received the name *London* and its present form in Playford's *Whole Book of Psalms* (1677). In 1816, 1940. For Psalm 33 (*NV*, cviii, sel. vv.). (*Comp.; Handbook.*)

No. 32. 5TH PSALM. Source not identified; perhaps Eckhard. In 1816. For Psalm 5 (*NV*, xvi, sel. vv.). Since only in Charleston would the sixteenth psalm of David be called "Psalm 5," it is very likely that this tune, *5th Psalm,* was written for this particular text, and is, therefore, of local origin.

No. 33. HARCOURT. Also in Charleston Museum Copy-book set to "How vast must their advantage be" (i.e., Psalm cxxxiii.). In 1816. For Psalm 37 (*NV*, cxxxiii).

No. 34. ST. PAUL'S. Valton. This tune may have been named for one of two rural parishes near Charleston. It appears also in the Charleston Museum Copy-book where it is attributed to Valton and set to Psalm ix. In 1816. For Psalm 3 (*NV*, ix, sel. vv.).

No. 35. ST. ANDREW'S. Valton. Probably named for the rural parish located just outside of Charleston or for St. Andrew's, Holborn, the mother parish of St. George's, Hanover Square, where Valton was organist. In 1816. For Psalm 13 (*NV*, xxxiii, sel. vv.).

No. 36. ST. JOHN'S OLD. Valton. In 1816. For Psalm 1 (*NV*, i, sel. vv.).

No. 37. ST. JAMES'S. First published in *Select Psalms and Hymns for Use of the Parish Church and Tabernacle of St. James, Westminster* (1697). Dr. Sander notes that it is by Raphael Courteville. In 1785, 1940. For Psalm 11 (*NV*, xxx, sel. vv.). (*Comp.*)

No. 38. CANTERBURY. One of the five new tunes written for Este's *Whole Booke of Psalms* (1592). In 1785. (Satcher.)

No. 39. COLESHILL. A cognate tune to *Windsor*. From Barton's *Psalter* (1644), Smith's *Psalms of David in Metre* (1706) (*Dublin Tune*), then *Collection of Psalm Tunes* (1711), Hopkinson (1763), and the proposed hymnal of 1785. (For the relationship between this tune and *Windsor,* see E. Routley, *The Music of Christian Hymnody* [London, 1957], pp. 48, 52, 209.) In 1785. This form of the tune does not appear in 1940, but the variant form from which it derived is found at number 284, *Windsor*. (Frost; *Comp.; Handbook;* Satcher.)

No. 40. ST. DAVID'S NEW. Though bearing a South Carolina name, this tune is the German chorale, "Nun sich der Tag geendet hat," composed by Adam Krieger and published in the *Darmstadter Gesangbuch* (1698). In 1816.

No. 41. WINDSOR. Hymn 40. A cognate tune to *Coleshill*. *Windsor* (or in Scotland, *Dundee*) may stem from Christopher Tye's *Acts of the Apostles* (1553). It appears in William Damon's *Former Booke* (1591), Este's *Whole Booke of Psalms* (1592), and four times in Ravenscroft, *Whole Booke of Psalmes* (1621). Attributed to Tans'ur in Pilsbury, *U. S. Sacred Harmony* (1799). In 1816, 1940. For Hymn 40, i.e., *NV*, xc, sel. vv. (*Comp.*)

No. 42. ST. MARGARET'S NEW. Heron. From Heron's *Parochial Music Corrected* (1790). For Hymn 8, i.e., *NV*, xxii, sel. vv.

No. 43. BEXLY. Appeared in Aaron Williams' *New Universal Psalmodist* (1770) set to Psalm lxxxiv. Also in the Charleston Museum Copy-book for "When Heaven thy beauteous work on high," i.e., Psalm viii. In 1816. For Psalm 2 (*NV*, viii, sel. vv.).

No. 44. CROWLE. An anonymous tune first published in James Green's *A Book of Psalmody* (1724). Called *Crowley* in Pilsbury, *U. S. Sacred Harmony* (1799). For Psalm 7 (*NV*, xxii, sel. vv.). (*Handbook.*)

No. 45. LIVERPOOL. This tune, composed by Robert Wainwright, organist of the church now the Liverpool Cathedral, was first printed in *Divine Harmony selected by R. Langdon* (1774); also in Pilsbury (1799). In 1816. For Psalm 8 (*NV*, xxiii, sel. vv.). (Supp.)

No. 46. ST. GEORGE's. Source not identified. One of the rural parishes near Charleston is St. George's.

No. 47. MEAR. Dr. Sander has discovered the first publication of this tune in this form (Form B, as he terms it) in *A Collection of Psalm Tunes for Gosport*, New Hampshire, not later than 1750. It was republished in Boston in 1757 for a new version of Tate and Brady and in 1793 in *American Harmony*. In 1785, 1816. For Psalm 14 (*NV*, xxxiv, sel. vv.). (Satcher.)

No. 48. FOSTER. From John Rippon's *Selection of Tunes* (1791) where it is attributed to Wilkins. In 1816. For Psalm 15 (*NV*, xlii, sel. vv.).

No. 49. POPLAR. Source not identified. For Psalm 15 (see note to 48).

No. 50. 15TH PSALM. Source not identified. This tune, like Numbers 48 and 49, could have been used for Psalm 15 (*NV*, xlii); if it was so used, then the fact that the name of the tune derives from the psalm number peculiar to the Charleston *Selection* would suggest a local origin for the tune.

No. 51. FLETTON. Source not identified. For Psalm 35 (*NV*, cxviii, sel. vv.).

No. 52. CHRIST CHURCH. This tune appears also in the Charleston Museum Copy-book where it accompanies Psalm cxlv. For Psalm 41 (*NV*, cxlv, sel. vv.). The fact that this tune (not otherwise identified) has the name of one of the rural parishes near Charleston and appears in the Museum Copy-book set to the same text from the 1792 *Selection* suggests that it is probably of local origin.

No. 53. ST. ANNE's OLD. This tune was composed by Dr. Croft for the 1708 *Supplement to the New Version* of Tate and Brady. It was omitted from the proposed hymnal of 1785 at the request of Dr. William Smith who considered it less popular than *Brunswick* or *Stroud;* "*St. Anne's*, though good, is too difficult for singers in gen-

eral." In 1816, 1940. For Psalm 42 (*NV*, cxlvi, sel. vv.). (*Handbook;* Satcher.)

No. 54. AMESBURY. In H. Heron's *Parochial Music Corrected* (London, 1790) and there attributed to Heron. In 1816. For Psalm 43 (*NV*, cxlvii, sel. vv.).

No. 55. BEDFORD. Published first in Playford's *Whole Book of Psalms* of 1677, adapted by William Weale, organist at Bedford. The time was changed generally to common time after 1812. In 1785, 1816, 1940. For Psalm 29 (*NV*, xcviii, sel. vv.) and, as a penciled afterthought, Hymn 40. (Supp.; *Handbook*.)

No. 56. MESSIAH. The opening phrases of the aria from Handel's *Messiah*, "I know that my Redeemer liveth." The tune was also known under the name *Bradford*, according to Dr. Sander. In 1816.

No. 57. NEWARK. Source not identified. For Hymn 22, author not identified.

No. 58. WESTMINSTER. By James Nares, first published in Riley's *Parochial Harmony* (1762) and classed as a new tune. For Hymn 25, i.e., *NV*, xli, sel. vv. (Lightwood.)

No. 59. GRANBY. In 1816 Eckhard confesses the origin of this locally named tune to be "Christus der ist mein Leben." This chorale is attributed to Vulpius in 1609. In 1816.

No. 60. ST. GEORGE's NEW. The German chorale "Nun danket all und bringet Ehr," also known as *Grafenberg* or *St. Mary Magdalen*, composed by Johann Crüger for *Praxis Pietatis Melica* (1653), 5th edition. Zahn 207. In 1816, 1940. (*Comp.*)

No. 61. IRISH. First published in Dublin in 1749 in S. Powell's *Hymns and Sacred Poems* and thought by some to be the work of John Wesley. It received this name in Caleb Ashworth's *Collection* (1760) where it was set to the folk song "The Cameronian Cat." In 1816, 1940. (*Comp.*; Supp.)
  Irish and *Abingdon* both appear, in reverse order, on p. 39 in Pilsbury, *U. S. Sacred Harmony* (1799), which suggests that Eckhard was copying from that book.

No. 62. ABINGDON. Attributed to Heighington in Pilsbury (1799). In 1816. See note to 61.

No. 63. PSALM 23. From the *Foundling Collection* (1774), where it is set to Psalm xxiii.

No. 64. ST. DAVID'S. Ravenscroft. From Ravenscroft's *Whole Booke of Psalmes* (1621). The present form is that of Playford's *Whole Book of Psalms* (1677). (*Handbook.*)

No. 65. PSALM CVIII. From the *Foundling Collection* (1774), where it is set to Psalm cviii.

No. 66. PSALM XV. From the *Foundling Collection* (1774), where it is set to Psalm xv.

No. 67. ST. MATTHEW'S. Dr. Croft. Another of Dr. Croft's tunes from the 1708 *Supplement to the New Version* of Tate and Brady. In 1785, 1816, 1940. For Psalm 10 (*NV,* xxvi, sel. vv.). (*Handbook.*)

No. 68. 21ST PSALM. Rev. Dr. Purcell. Though no assignment appears, this tune was probably for Psalm 21 (*NV,* lxxxvi, sel. vv.); Psalm xxi of David is not included in the Charleston *Selection* of 1792.

No. 69. 21ST HYMN. Dr. Purcell. Though no assignment appears, this tune was probably for Hymn 21, a selection of verses from hymns of Philip Doddridge, *Hymns* (1755). It might even be argued that Purcell, who had arranged the text of this hymn, composed the tune especially for it, as there are significant parallels between the textual images and the musical setting—e.g., the high notes for "to bear our souls above," and the low for "damp."

No. 70. 27TH HYMN. Dr. Sander identifies this as *Old 81st* from Day's *Whole Booke of Psalmes* (1562). For Hymn 27, by Anna Barbauld from W. Enfield's *Hymns* (1772). See also note to Anthem [I].

No. 71. BOSTON. Appeared first in *American Harmony* (1769) where it is called "A New Hymn for Christmas Day," attributed to A. W. (Aaron Williams). Eckhard retains the music for the concluding antiphonal hallelu-jahs, though his text does not include them. For Hymn 30, by Joseph Addison, *Spectator,* No. 453 (August 9, 1712).

No. 85. See in proper numerical order. It should be noted that this is the last of the numbered tunes. It is numbered out of place, as if by afterthought or a late discovery. The style of writing for the number is quite different from that of all other numbers, thus further marking its distinctness.

No. 72. PECKHAM. Appears also in James Steven's *Selection* (Glasgow, 1801). The notation "S. M." (Short Meter, 66.86.) that appears at the head of this tune applies to tunes 72–76A. The meter is used in the *Selection* of 1792 by Psalms 17 and 19 only, specified in tunes 72 and 73. In 1816. For Psalm 17 (*NV,* li, sel. vv.).

No. 73. MOUNT EPHRAIM. This tune first appears in *Sixteen Hymns as they are sung at the Right Honorable the Countess of Huntingdon's Chapel at Bath* (1769). It is by B. Milgrove. See preceding note. In 1816. For Psalm 19 (*NV,* lxvii, sel. vv.). (*Handbook.*)

No. 74. ST. SIMON'S. From *American Harmony* (1769). In 1816.

No. 75. AYLESBURY. Appears first in Chetham, *Book of Psalmody* (1718), the third phrase slightly different. Present form first published in James Green's *Book of Psalm Tunes* (1724). Appears also in *American Harmony* (1793) and in Pilsbury, *U. S. Sacred Harmony* (1799), in both of which it is attributed to Aaron Williams. In 1816.

No. 76. ALL SAINTS. Dr. Howard. This tune, composed by Dr. Samuel Howard, was published in 1762 under the name *St. Bride.* It received the name used by Eckhard in Edward Miller's *Psalms of David* (1790). In 1940. (*Comp.*)

[No. 76A.] PENTONVILLE. Linley. This tune is doubtless the work of Francis Linley, the blind organist of St. James' Chapel, Pentonville, London. See also Anthem [III].

No. 77. NEW COURT. In Pilsbury, *U. S. Sacred Harmony* (1799) and in Samuel Holyoke's *Columbian Repository* (1809) where it is attributed to Hugh Bond. In 1816. For Psalm 24 (*NV*, xci, sel. vv.).

No. 78. ST. MARK's. Valton. St. Mark's Parish was one of the large parishes in the interior of South Carolina. For Psalm 16 (*NV*, l, sel. vv.).

No. 79. LENOX. Perhaps the most popular and certainly the longest-lived of the American "fuguing tunes," *Lenox* was composed by Lewis Edson and first printed in *The Chorister's Companion* (1782–83), as Dr. Sander has noted. Also in Pilsbury, *U. S. Sacred Harmony* (1799). In 1816.

No. 80. [   ]. This tune is from the *Foundling Collection* (1774), where it is set to Psalm cxlviii. The text provided is Psalm 44 (*NV*, cxlviii, sel. vv.). See also note to 82.

No. 81. 149 PSALM PROPER. Handel. This tune is from the 1708 *Supplement to the New Version* of Tate and Brady where it is headed "A New Tune to the 149th Psalm of the New Version." It received the name *Hanover* in Gawthorne's *Harmonia Perfecta* (1730). The attribution to Handel is common in the eighteenth century though without foundation; Croft is now generally regarded as the composer. Also in Charleston Museum Copy-book where it is attributed to Handel and accompanies Psalm cxlix. In 1785, 1816, 1940. For Psalm 45 (the text provided) (*NV*, cxlix, sel. vv.). (*Handbook;* Satcher; *Comp.*)

No. 82. 148 PSALM PROPER. DARWALL's. *Foundling Collection* (1774). Composed by John Darwall for Psalm cxlviii for Aaron Williams' *New Universal Psalmodist* (1770). In 1940. Text provided is Psalm 44; see note to 80. (*Comp.*)

No. 83. KENT. George Green. The composer of *Kent* is generally thought to have been Johann Friedrich Lampe, though the attribution to Dr. Green is found also in *Evangelical Music* (1834) and in Nahum Mitchell's *Templi Carmina* (1812), as Dr. Sander has observed. These versions are much simplified from that of the

tune as it first appeared in Charles Wesley's *Hymns on the Great Festivals and other Occasions* (1746). Numbers 83 and 84 follow the tunes of miscellaneous meters and are the last Long Meter tunes in the numbered sequence. (*Handbook.*)

No. 84. MADAN's. Attributed to C. Lockhart, organist at the Lock Chapel, in Rippon's *Selection of Tunes* (1791). The setting for Psalm 28 is awkward, as the music provides six lines for the text's four; some adjustment would have to be made in actual use. Psalm xxviii of David is not represented in the *Selection* of 1792. For Psalm 28 (*NV*, xcvii, sel. vv.). See note to 83.

No. 85 (*located after* 71). BURFORD. Purcell. A minor tune, *Burford* is included in Chetham's *Book of Psalmody* (1718) but is first named in Gawthorne's *Harmonia Perfecta* (1730). The attribution to Purcell, though customary in the nineteenth century, is without foundation. Edward Miller, *Psalms of David* (1790), heads the tune, "said to be Purcell's." *Grove's* as late as 1927 lists it among Purcell's works. In 1940. The tune is the last of the Common Meter tunes in the numbered sequence. (*Handbook*, Supp.)

[No. i.] *Vital Spark*. In Pilsbury, *U. S. Sacred Harmony* (1799), called "The Dying Christian." The text provided is Hymn 45, by Alexander Pope (*ca.* 1712). The presence of the extra "Hark" above the line on the third staff is derived from the three-part harmony as given, for example, in Pilsbury. In 1816.

[No. ii.] *Hymn for Easter*. In *Foundling Collection* (1774). The basic tune (*Easter Hymn*, in 1940) appeared in *Lyra Davidica* (1708). The setting occurs also in the Charleston Museum Copy-book, called "Hymn for Easter." The text provided is from John Arnold's *Compleat Psalmodist* (1749); see also Hymn 9 (*Selection* of 1792).

The four stanzas of alternate text supplied below the music of *Hymn for Easter* are also intended for use with this setting. These verses, of unknown authorship and evidently intended as a paraphrase of Psalm cxlviii, were associated with the Foundling Hospital. They were first printed in 1801 and then assigned to music by Haydn. (See essay on this text in Julian's *Dictionary*.)

[No. a.] *Chaunt*. Source not identified.

[No. b.] *Chaunt single*. Source not identified.

[No. c.] *Chaunt double*. Source not identified. Used for [k] below.

[No. d.] *Chaunt single*. Source not identified. Used for [m] below.

[No. e.] *Chaunt single*. Source not identified.

[No. f.] *Chaunt single*. Found also in 1785.

[No. g.] *Chaunt single*. Source not identified. In 1816, page 69.

[No. h.] *Chaunt*. "O come let us sing unto the Lord." The *Venite*, a conflated canticle consisting of verses from Psalms xcv and xcvi, prepared for the American *Book of Common Prayer* (1789) to replace Psalm xcv sung in the Church of England (see the rubric on p. 8 of modern editions of the prayer book). (*Comp.*)

[No. ij.] [   ]. An alternate setting, double chant, for the *Venite*.

[No. k.] *Chaunt double*. Source not identified. "Benedic, anima mea" (verses from Psalm ciii). See [c] above. In 1816, pages 6, 72.

[No. 86.] VANHALL'S GERMAN HYMN. By John Baptist Wanhall, this melody is the theme of a set of variations published first in John Bland's *Second Collection of Sonatas, Lessons, Overtures, &c for the Harpsichord or Piano Forte* (London, 1790). In 1816. The text provided is the first verse of Psalm 6 (*NV*, xviii, sel. vv.). In 1816 the text provided is the first verse of Psalm 32 (*NV*, cvi, sel. vv.).

[No. l.] *Jubilate Deo*. Source not identified. In 1816. A special setting for the chant (Psalm c).

[No. m.] *Deus misereatur*. Source not identified. "Deus misereatur" (Psalm lxvii). See [d] above.

[No. n.] *Chaunt*. Source not identified.

[No. 87.] SICILIAN MARINER'S HYMN. First published in Philadelphia in *The Gentleman's Amusement* (1794), an Italian folk song or operatic air. In 1940. The text provided is that of the Eighth *Gloria Patri* in the *Selection* of 1792. (*Comp.*)

[No. 88.] SOUTHWELL. Source not identified. For Psalm 4 (*NV*, xv, sel. vv.).

[No. 89.] NOTTINGHAM. Source not identified. For Psalm 9 (*NV*, xxiv, sel. vv.).

[No. 90.] GRANTHAM. Source not identified. For Psalm 20 (*NV*, lxxxiv, sel. vv.).

[No. 91.] HOMECASTLE. Source not identified. For Psalm 25 (*NV*, xciii).

[No. 92.] SLEAFORD. Source not identified. For Psalm 26 (*NV*, xcv, sel. vv.).

[No. 93.] ST. LUKE'S. Mr. Theodore M. Finney, curator of the Warrington Hymnological Collection, has pointed out a slightly variant version of this tune in *Church Tunes in four parts* (Perth: D. Peat, 1801). For Psalm 32 (*NV*, cvi, sel. vv.).

[No. 94.] HORNBY. Source not identified. For Hymn 11, by Tate and Brady, *Supplement to the New Version* (1702).

[No. 95.] WHITTLESEA. Source not identified. For Psalm 36 (*NV*, cxix, sel. vv.).

[No. 96.] LINCOLN. Source not identified. For Hymn 10, stanzas 4–5 of a hymn by Isaac Watts published in *Horæ Lyricæ* (1709), altered in Madan's *Psalms and Hymns* (1760). The second stanza is anonymous.

[No. 97.] [   ]. Source not identified. For Hymn 15, i.e., *NV*, xxiv, sel. vv.

[No. 98.] [   ]. Source not identified. For Hymn 32, by Joseph Addison, *Spectator,* No. 441 (July 26, 1712), a paraphrase of Psalm xxiii.

[No. 99.] PETERBOROUGH. Source not identified. For Hymn 33, by Philip Doddridge, *Hymns* (1755).

[No. 100.] EVENING HYMN. Source not identified. The text provided is the first verse of Hymn 47, by an anonymous author. The remainder of the text for that hymn is Bishop Thomas Ken's "Evening Hymn" (1709), which concludes with the familiar doxology that follows here under the heading "Gloria Patri." The text provided is that of the Third *Gloria Patri* in the *Selection* of 1792, rather than that of Hymn 47, but the only difference is the phrase "ye heav'nly host" in place of Ken's "the angelic host." See [iii] below.

[No. iii.] *Gloria Patri.* See [100] above. A special choral setting of the doxology. It is possible that *Evening Hymn* and *Gloria Patri* were sung as a unit, without the interpolation of Bishop Ken's stanzas. Such an arrangement would be appropriate at a service of evening prayer. At the same time, the opening stanza appropriately introduces the bishop's text.

[No. 101.] [   ]. Source not identified. For Hymn 16, by Charles Wesley, *Collection* (1743). The tune which accompanies two verses of the text requires the repetition of the last line of the second verse. The assignment is awkward in that it provides music for only four of the five verses in the *Selection,* but an adjustment could of course be made.

[No. 102.] 29TH HYMN. Source not identified. For Hymn 29(?); see note to [104].

[No. 103.] [   ]. Source not identified. "Short Metre"; see note to 72.

[No. o.] *Christmas Day.* Source not identified. The text provided is the opening phrase of Psalm lxxxi (version in the *Book of Common Prayer*). This and perhaps [p] are the only examples in this collection of chanting the psalms by Anglican chant, though the specific canticles that are psalms are set in numbers [h, ij, k, l, m].

[No. p.] *New Years Day.* Source not identified.

[No. q.] *Chaunt.* Unitas Fratrum. A chant for the *Te Deum Laudamus* in the Moravian Litany, slightly altered from the original. First published in English in C. I. Latrobe, *Hymn-Tunes sung in the Church of the United Brethren* (London, 1806). See [r] below.

[No. r.] [   ]. Unitas Fratrum. Composed by Bishop Christian Gregor (1763) and published in his *Choral-Buch* (Leipzig, 1784) as "Die Gnade unsers Herrn Jesu Christi." First published in English in Latrobe, *Hymn-Tunes* (1806). See [q] above. I am indebted to Dr. Donald McCorkle for the information on these two Moravian chants.

[No. 104.] HYMN 29TH. T. Welsh. Source not identified. The text provided is Hymn 29, by an anonymous author. It is a text for Thanksgiving Day and was probably written by an American. See also [102].

[No. 105.] A FAVORITE GERMAN HYMN. The chorale "Wer nun den lieben Gott lässt walten," attributed to Georg Neumark. *Bach Gesellschaft,* xxii, 94. See also 17. Long Meter.

[No. 106.] GLORIA PATRI. Source not identified. The text provided is the Second *Gloria Patri* in the *Selection* of 1792.

[No. iv.] *Hymn for Easter.* Source not identified. The text provided is Hymn 13, by an unidentified author. The curious metrical shift of this text—7 lines of 11 syllables, then 4 stanzas of Long Meter—requires a special setting; only Hymns 9 (no tune provided) and 45 ([i]) share this sort of shift. The composer has pictorially represented the "gushing rill."

[No. 107.] ORANGE. The source of this tune has not been identified. Dr. Sander has, however, pointed to a similar or cognate tune first printed in Wyeth's *Repository of Sacred Music. Part Second* (Harrisburg, 1813; facsimile ed. by Irving Lowens, New York, 1964) which, though differing rhythmically, is almost identical melodically. The tune is attributed to Chapin, presumably Amzi Chapin (1768–1835), a singing-master active in Virginia and North Carolina in the early 1790s. The tune is called *Twenty-fourth* in the *Repository* (p. 20); and it is also included, under the name *Primrose,* in all of the six leading Southern collections of folk hymn tunes published between 1815 and 1844 that derive from Wyeth. Only one other of the fifty-eight folk hymn tunes in the *Repository* enjoyed such popularity (Lowens' edition, pp. viii–ix). Dr. Ellinwood writes: "My own feeling is that . . . *Orange* is in the traditional idiom [and *Twenty-fourth* and *Primrose*] . . . are folk idiom. It is just as likely that [*Twenty-fourth* is adapted from] *Orange* as the other way around."

[No. s.] *Gloria in Excelsis.* In 1816, pages 7, 76–77, where it is attributed to "J. Eckhard, sen."

[No. t.] [   ]. The text provided for this chant was used before the reading of the Gospel at Holy Communion.

[No. u.] [   ]. A setting of the acclamation (see [t]).

[No. 108.] PSALM 63. Dr. Sander has identified this as deriving from *Old 124th* or *Toulon,* originally by L. Bourgeois for the *Genevan Psalter* (1551). The text provided is that of Psalm lxiii in the *New Version* of Tate and Brady. This text presents a unique problem in the collection, for it is the only psalm text not included in the forty-six psalms of the *Selection* of 1792. *New Court* is at No. 77; the meter is 88.88.88.

[No. 109.] MARTIN'S LANE. In Pilsbury, *U. S. Sacred Harmony* (1799). In 1816.

[No. 110.] KOMMT HER ZU MIR SPRICHT GOTTES SOHN. The tune is the German chorale; Zahn 2496. In 1816. *New Court* is at No. 77; the meter is 88.88.88.

[No. 111.] [   ]. Double Tune. Source not identified. The meter is Common Meter doubled.

[No. I.] *Anthem.* This charity anthem is almost certainly by Eckhard. The text provided is one of the offertory sentences from the *Book of Common Prayer,* followed by Hymn 27 from the *Selection,* altered from Anna Barbauld's hymn in W. Enfield, *Hymns* (1772). See also note to 70.

[No. II.] *Anthem.* A charity anthem probably by Eckhard. There would seem to be alternate codas for this anthem. The text has not been identified.

[No. III.] *Christmas Hymn.* F. Lindley. The anthem, by Francis Linley, is taken from Bland's *Collection of Divine Music,* No. 12 (London, 1790).

[No. IV.] *Anthem for Christmas Day.* C. Bond. The anthem is taken from Capel Bond, *Six Anthems in Score* (London, 1769). The text provided beneath the heading "Brunswic" is probably by Madan, having been first published in his *Psalms and Hymns* (1760). It is also found in slightly different form as Hymn 4.

[No. V.] *Anthem for the Fourth of July.* Probably by Eckhard. The text provided after the *maestoso* introduction is Hymn 35, stanzas 1–2 from *NV,* Psalm lxxxi (see also [o]), stanzas 3–5 by an unidentified author, perhaps Dr. Purcell.

Biographical Notices of Composers Cited by Eckhard

Note: Tunes in brackets are the work of the composer indicated though not ascribed to him in the manuscript.

Bond, C[apel] (d. 1790?). Organist and composer of Coventry. Author of *Six Concertos* (1766) and *Six Anthems in Score* (1769). (*Grove's.*)

  IV *Anthem for Christmas Day*

Cook, [Benjamin, Jr.,] Mr. (1734–93). Organist and composer of London. Organist of Westminster Abbey and St. Martin-in-the-Fields. Doctor of Music at Cambridge and at Oxford. His numerous compositions are "for church, concert-room, and chamber" and include "a few hymn tunes." (*Grove's;* Frost.)

  27 PSALM 8TH.

Croft, [William,] Dr. (1678–1727). Organist and composer of London. Organist of Westminster Abbey. Doctor of Music at Oxford. Composer of many anthems and much service music; published *Musica Sacra* (1724) in two volumes. Composer of the following three psalm tunes of permanent value, which appeared in the *Supplement to the New Version* (1708). (*Grove's; Comp.*)

  67 ST. MATTHEW'S
  [53 ST. ANNE'S OLD]
  [81 149 PSALM PROPER (HANOVER)]

Green, George. Not identified. Attribution erroneous.

  83 KENT

Handel, [George Frederick] (1685–1759). Born in Halle, moved to London in 1712. Composer of many operas and sacred oratorios. The best known, *Messiah,* was written in 1742.

  81 149 PSALM PROPER (Attribution erroneous; see Croft.)
  [56 MESSIAH]

Heron, H. Organist at St. Magnus, London Bridge, and compiler of *Parochial Music Corrected* (1790).

  42 ST. MARGARET'S NEW
  [54 AMESBURY]

Howard, [Samuel,] Dr. (1710?–1782). Organist and composer of London. Organist at St. Clement Danes and St. Bride, Fleet Street. Doctor of Music at Cambridge. Composer of music for theater; assisted Boyce in the preparation of *Cathedral Music* (1760–78). (*Grove's.*)

  76 ALL SAINTS

Linley, F[rancis] (1771–1800). Organist, music dealer, and composer of London and Doncaster. Blind from birth, he became the able organist of St. James's Chapel, Pentonville, London. Visited America 1796–99 where his playing and compositions were much admired. (*Grove's.*)

76A PENTONVILLE
III *Christmas Hymn*

Purcell, [Henry] (1659–95). Organist and composer of London. Organist of Westminster Abbey and composer of many operas, cantatas, and secular pieces. Though *Burford* has been ascribed to Purcell since 1790, there is no contemporary evidence to support the ascription. It is not upheld by Frost or the *Companion*. (Frost; *Comp.*)

85 BURFORD

Purcell, Rev. Dr. [Henry] (1742–1802). Priest and composer of Charleston. Born in Hereford, educated at Christ Church College, Oxford; ordained priest in 1768, officiated at Great and Little Warley, Essex 1766–70. (John Arnold, compiler of the popular *Compleat Psalmodist,* was organist there at the time.) Then he emigrated to South Carolina where he officiated at St. George's, Dorchester, and Christ Church Parish 1771–78, and was chaplain to the Second South Carolina Regiment during the Revolutionary War. Rector of St. Michael's Church, 1784–1802. Delegate to the General Convention of 1785 and member of the committee appointed to revise the Book of Common Prayer. Compiler, with Bishop Smith, of the *Selection of Psalms with Occasional Hymns,* certified in Charleston in 1792; probably arranger of some of the *New Version* psalms and possibly author of some of the hymns. Composer of psalm and hymn tunes, five of which are preserved by Eckhard. That these tunes "were set down in 1809, seven years after his death, shows that in his time they were considered memorable." See G. W. Williams, "Henry Purcell," *Early Ministers at St. Michael's* (Charleston: Dalcho Historical Society, 1961); and L. Ellinwood, ed., *The Charleston Hymnal of 1792* (Charleston: Dalcho Historical Society, 1956).

11 ST. MICHAEL'S NEW
25 HEREFORD
26 OXFORD
68 21ST PSALM
69 21ST HYMN

Ravenscroft, [Thomas] (1592?–1635?). Theorist, editor, and composer of London. Compiler or editor of *Pammelia: Musick's Miscellanie* (1609), *Deuteromelia: or the Second Part . . .* (1609), *Melismata* (1611), *A Brief Discourse of the true . . . use of Charact'ring the Degrees . . . in . . . Musicke* (1614); his most important work, *The Whole Booke of Psalmes* (1621), contained forty-eight tune harmonizations by him, though apparently no original tunes. (*Grove's.*)

64 ST. DAVID'S

Stevens, J[ervis] H[enry] (1750–1828). Postmaster, coroner, sheriff, organist, and composer of Charleston. Born in London, he came to Georgia about 1760. In 1766 his father, John Stevens, presented the first concert known to have been given in Savannah. Shortly afterward the family moved to Charleston where John served as organist of St. Michael's 1768–72. Jervis Henry became deputy postmaster for Charleston in 1772 and held that office until he volunteered for service with Col. Maham's Cavalry as a captain. Organist at St. Michael's 1783–84, and at St. Philip's 1790–1815. Coroner for Charleston District 1802–22; city sheriff 1801–20. Composer of two tunes preserved by Eckhard. (G. W. Williams, "Eighteenth-century Organists of St. Michael's," *S. C. Hist. Mag.,* LIII [1952], 150–52, 216–20.)

20 HACKNEY
24 CHURCH STREET

Valton, [Peter] 1740?–84). Organist and composer of London and Charleston. Deputy organist at King's Chapel, Westminster Abbey, and St. George's, Hanover Square, studied with Dr. Boyce and Dr. Nares in London; emigrated to Charleston 1764 to take the post of organist at St. Philip's, which post he held until 1781 when he moved to St. Michael's during the British occupation of the city; he remained at that bench until 1783. Composer of many catches, glees, and a song, "The Reprisal," sung at Marybone Gardens (1765), as well as the psalm tunes preserved by Eckhard. Teacher of harpsichord, music dealer, active in the musical life of the city. (G. W. Williams, "Eighteenth-century Organists of St. Michael's," *S. C. Hist. Mag.,* LIII [1952], 212–16).

1 ST. PETER'S
2 ST. PHILIP'S
4 ST. MICHAEL'S
5 ST. ANN'S NEW
[22, 23 MAGDALEN]
34 ST. PAUL'S

35 ST. ANDREW'S
36 ST. JOHN'S OLD
78 ST. MARK'S

Welsh, T. This is possibly the Thomas Welsh (c. 1780–1848) cited in *Grove's*. Though best known as a singer and composer of popular dramatic songs, he was chorister boy and man in Bath and London and achieved a notable reputation in that capacity. (The Card Catalog of the Music Division, Library of Congress, gives his birth as 1770.)

104 HYMN 29TH

Selective List
of Works Consulted

A. Critical and Historical

Benson, Louis F. *The English Hymn*. New York: Hodder & Stoughton, [1915].

Blom, Eric, ed. *Grove's Dictionary of Music and Musicians*. 5th ed. London: Macmillan & Co., Ltd., 1954. [*Grove's*]

Ellinwood, Leonard. *The Charleston Hymnal of 1792*. Charleston: Dalcho Historical Society, 1956.

Foote, Henry Wilder. *Three Centuries of American Hymnody*. Cambridge, Mass.: Harvard University Press, 1940.

Frost, Maurice, ed. *Historical Companion to Hymns Ancient & Modern*. London: William Clowes & Sons, Ltd., [1962]. [*Frost*]

The Hymnal 1940 Companion. (Prepared by the Joint Commission on the Revision of the Hymnal.) New York: The Church Pension Fund, 1949. [*Comp.*]

Julian, John. *Dictionary of Hymnology*. London: John Murray, [1892].

Lightwood, James T. *The Music of the Methodist Hymn-book*. London: Epworth Press, 1935. Rev. ed., 1955. [*Lightwood*]

McCutchan, Robert Guy. *Hymn Tune Names: Their Sources and Significance*. New York & Nashville: Abingdon Press, [1957].

Macdougall, Hamilton C. *Early New England Psalmody: An Historical Appreciation, 1620–1820*. Brattleboro, Vt.: Stephen Daye Press, [1940].

Martin, Hugh, ed. *A Companion to the Baptist Church Hymnal*. Rev. ed. London: Psalms and Hymns Trust, [1962].

Metcalf, Frank J. *American Psalmody or Titles of Books, Containing Tunes, Printed in America from 1721 to 1820*. New York: Charles F. Heartman, 1917.

————. *American Writers and Compilers of Sacred Music*. Nashville: Abingdon Press, 1925.

Moffatt, James, ed. *Handbook to The Church Hymnary*. London: Humphrey Milford, 1927. [*Handbook*]

Patrick, Millar, ed. Supplement to the *Handbook to the Church Hymnary etc.* London: Oxford University Press, 1935. [*Supp.*]

Polack, W. G. *The Handbook to the Lutheran Hymnal*. St. Louis: Concordia, [1942].

Protestant Episcopal Church. *Book of Common Prayer*. Charleston: W. P. Young, 1799.

Satcher, Herbert Boyce. "Music of the Episcopal Church in Pennsylvania in the Eighteenth Century," *Historical Magazine of the Protestant Episcopal Church*, XVIII (December 1949), 372–413. [*Satcher*]

Shepherd, Massey H. *The Oxford American Prayer Book Commentary*. New York: Oxford University Press, [1950].

Zahn, Johannes. *Die Melodien der deutschen evangelischen Kirchen lieder*. 6 vols. Gutersloh, 1889–93.

B. Collections of Tunes and Texts

I. MANUSCRIPT

Music for the Lute. A Copy-book in the Charleston Museum (Museum Collection 26709).

The provenience of this manuscript is unrecorded. It contains a reference to a book published in 1820 and is therefore at least that late. Its contents of various musical pieces testify to the fact that Valton's tunes were still known as set to the texts of the *Selection* of 1792, eleven years after Eckhard wrote them down.

2. PRINTED COLLECTIONS

Buist, George, ed. *A Version of the Book of Psalms . . . A Collection of Hymns for public and private worship. . . .* Charleston: J. MacIver, 1796.

Eckhard, Jacob, Senior, organist of St. Michael's. *Choral-Book, containing Psalms, Hymns, Anthems and Chants used in the Episcopal Churches of Charleston, South Carolina; and a collection of tunes, adapted to the Metres in the Hymn-Book, published by order of the Evangelical Lutheran Synod of the State of New York. The whole a selection for the service of all protestant churches in America.* Boston: printed by James Loring, for the Author. [1816].

Hopkinson, Francis. *A Collection of Psalm Tunes, with a Few Anthems and Hymns. . . .* [Philadelphia: Dunlap, 1763].

Lyon, James, *Urania.* Philadelphia, 1761–62.

Madan, Martin. *A Collection of Psalms and Hymns Extracted from Various Authors.* (The Lock Collection for the use of the Chapel of the Lock Hospital.) Compiled by M. Madan. [London, 1769].

    A copy of this collection, now in the Charleston Library Society, was acquired by Col. and Mrs. Barnard Elliott in 1774; Col. Elliott was the brother-in-law of the Rev. William Percy, minister at St. Michael's 1777–80, 1805–09.

Pilsbury, Amos, *United States' Sacred Harmony. Containing . . . a large and valuable Collection of Psalm Tunes and Anthems. Selected from the most celebrated Authors in the United States and Great Britain. For the Use of Schools, Singing Societies, and Churches. Also,—A Large Number of Tunes Never Before Published.* Boston: Thomas & Andrews, Nov. 1799. (Sold also in Charleston, S. C., where the compiler lived.)

Protestant Episcopal Church. *Book of Common Prayer . . . [with] Tunes suited to the Psalms and Hymns. . . .* Philadelphia: Hall and Sellers, 1786. [the "proposed hymnal of 1785"]

———. *A Selection of Psalms with Occasional Hymns.* Charleston: W. P. Young, [1792?] [1799].

———. *A Selection of Psalm Tunes for the Use of the Protestant Episcopal Church in the State of New York.* New York: Swords, 1812.

Psalms, Hymns and Anthems used in the Chapel of the Hospital for . . . Deserted Young Children. London, 1774. [*Foundling Collection*]

Tate, Nahum, and Brady, Nicholas. *A New Version of the Psalms of David fitted to the Tunes used in Churches.* London: M. Clark, 1696. [*NV*]

Appendix

A

SELECTION

OF

PSALMS,

WITH

OCCASIONAL

HYMNS.

CHARLESTON:
PRINTED FOR W. P. YOUNG,
43,
BROAD-STREET.

FACSIMILE OF TITLE PAGE OF
CHARLESTON *Selection* OF 1792

The Charleston
Selection of 1792

A Selection of Psalms with Occasional Hymns (Charleston: Printed for W. P. Young, 43 Broad-Street) was published under this certificate (on the verso of the title page):

WE hereby certify, That the following SELECTION *of* PSALMS *and* HYMNS, *is a true Copy from the Original in our Hands.*

ROBERT SMITH,
Rector of St. Philip's Church.

HENRY PURCELL,
Rector of St. Michael's Church.

Charleston, Nov. 10, 1792.

No copies of an edition of 1792 are known to exist; all extant copies are bound with the edition of the 1789 *Book of Common Prayer*, printed in Charleston in 1799 (Evans 36175). The edition of the *Selection* is conjunct with the prayer book and like the prayer book printed on paper with a watermark date of 1796. The extant copies cannot therefore have existed before that date, and they certainly date from 1799. The *Selection* has been republished in facsimile under the title *The Charleston Hymnal of 1792* (Charleston: Dalcho Historical Society, 1956) with an Introduction by Leonard Ellinwood describing the making of the *Selection* and tracing the sources of the hymns.

As Dr. Ellinwood points out in that Introduction, Smith and Purcell rearranged extensively the stanzas of the forty-six *New Version* psalms they included. These changes are scrupulously recorded at the head of each psalm selection. They made similar though less sweeping changes to the stanzas of the hymns which they assembled, drawn principally from such nonconformist authors as Watts, Doddridge, Charles Wesley, and Samuel J. Smith. The ten doxologies at the conclusion derive from various sources. Interestingly, seven of them appear also in the parallel collection of psalms and hymns compiled by the Reverend George Buist for the Charleston Presbytery and published in Charleston in 1796.

The lists that follow give the contents of the *Selection:* the selections from the psalms as adapted from the *New Version* of Tate and Brady, the first lines of the hymns, and the first lines of the doxologies.

Psalms

Psalm No.	*New Version*	Set at Eckhard No.
1	*from* Psalm i. Verses 1, 2, 3, 6.	36
2	*from* Psalm viii. Verses 3, 4, 5, 6, 9.	43
3	*from* Psalm ix. Verses 1, 2, 10, 12.	34
4	*from* Psalm xv. Verses 1, 2, 3, 4, 5, 7.	88
5	*from* Psalm xvi. Verses 8, 9, 10 11.	32
6	*from* Psalm xviii. Verses 1, 2, 6, 25, 26.	3, 86
7	*from* Psalm xxii. Verses 23, 24, 29.	47
8	*from* Psalm xxiii. Verses 1, 2, 3, 4, 6.	45, 27?
9	*from* Psalm xxiv. Verses 1, 3, 4, 5.	89
10	*from* Psalm xxvi. Verses 6, 7, 8, 9, 10, 11.	67
11	*from* Psalm xxx. Verses 1, 2, 3, 4, 5, 12.	37
12	*from* Psalm xxxii. Verses 1, 2, 8, 10, 11.	2
13	*from* Psalm xxxiii. Verses 1, 2, 3, 8, 9, 11.	35
14	*from* Psalm xxxiv. Verses 1, 2, 3, 4, 5, 9.	47
15	*from* Psalm xlii. Verses 1, 2, 5, 11.	48, 49, 50?
16	*from* Psalm l. Verses 1, 2, 3, 4, 7, 8, 13, 14.	78
17	*from* Psalm li. Verses 1, 2, 3, 8, 17, 7.	72

Psalm No.	*New Version*	Set at Eckhard No.
18	*from* Psalm lvii. Verses 7, 8, 9, 10, 11.	7
19	*from* Psalm lxvii. Verses 1, 2, 3, 4, 6.	73
20	*from* Psalm lxxxiv. Verses 4, 5, 6, 7.	90
21	*from* Psalm lxxxvi. Verses 1, 2, 3, 4, 5, 9, 10.	68?
22	*from* Psalm lxxxviii. Verses 1, 2, 7, 15, 12, 14.	8
23	*from* Psalm lxxxix. Verses 6, 7, 8, 9, 11, 13, 14.	25, 63?
24	*from* Psalm xci. Verses 1, 2, 3, 4, 5, 6.	77
25	Psalm xciii.	91
26	*from* Psalm xcv. Verses 1, 2, 6, 3.	92
27	*from* Psalm xcvi. Verses 1, 2, 3, 10, 11, 12, 13.	26
28	*from* Psalm xcvii. Verses 1, 2, 10, 11, 12.	84?
29	*from* Psalm xcviii. Verses 1, 2, 4, 9.	55
30	Psalm c.	9
31	*from* Psalm ciii. Verses 1, 2, 4, 8, 11.	6
32	*from* Psalm cvi. Verses 1, 2, 3, 4.	20, 93
33	*from* Psalm cviii. Verses 1, 2, 3, 4, 5.	31
34	*from* Psalm cxiii. Verses 1, 2, 3, 4, 5.	*none*
35	*from* Psalm cxviii. Verses 20, 21, 22, 23, 24, 25, 27.	51
36	*from* Psalm cxix, Verses 1, 2, 3, 4, 5, 6.	95
36	Part II, Verses 9, 10, 11, 18.	95
37	Psalm cxxxiii.	33
38	*from* Psalm cxxxiv. Verses 1, 4, 5, 6, 25, 26.	*none*
39	*from* Psalm cxxxvii. Verses 1, 2, 3, 4, 5, 6.	4
40	*from* Psalm cxxxix. Verses 1, 2, 3, 4, 5, 6, 12, 23, 24.	22
40	Part II, Verses 17, 18, 7, 8, 9, 10, 11.	23

Psalm No.	*New Version*	Set at Eckhard No.
41	*from* Psalm cxlv. Verses 1, 2, 3, 4, 5, 6.	52
42	*from* Psalm cxlvi. Verses 1, 2, 6, 7, 8, 9, 5.	53
43	*from* Psalm cxlvii. Verses 1, 3, 4, 5, 6, 7.	54
44	*from* Psalm cxlviii. Verses 1, 2, 5, 6, 13.	80, 82
45	*from* Psalm cxlix. Verses 1, 2, 3, 4.	81
46	Psalm cl.	1

HYMNS

Hymn No.	First Line	Set at Eckhard No.
1	While shepherds watch'd their flocks by night,	*none*
2	While angels thus, O Lord, rejoice,	*none*
3	The Lord is come; the heavens proclaim	*none*
4	Come let us all unite to praise	IV
5	Whilst tending on their fleecy care,	*none*
6	From whence these direful omens round,	*none*
7	Now let our mournful song record	*none*
8	My God, my God, why leav'st thou me,	42
9	He dies, the friend of sinners dies;	ii (in part)
10	The rising God forsakes the tomb,	96
11	Since Christ our passover is slain,	94
12	Plung'd in a gulph of dark despair,	*none*
13	To souls just perishing on the stormy deep	iv
14	To God, the universal King,	*none*
15	Erect your heads, eternal gates,	97
16	Our Lord is risen from the dead,	101
17	He's come! let ev'ry knee be bent,	*none*
18	Come, Holy Spirit, Heav'nly Dove,	*none*

Hymn No.	First Line	Set at Eckhard No.
19	O Lord, thy mercy, my sure hope,	*none*
20	My God, and is thy table spread?	11
21	And are we now brought near to God,	69
22	Wherewith shall I approach the Lord,	57
23	The God of life, whose constant care	*none*
24	Rise my soul, and stretch thy wings	29
25	Happy the man, whose tender care	58
26	The soul that's fill'd with virtue's light,	5
27	Blest is the man, whose soft'ning heart	70, I
28	Father of mercy! hear our pray'r	*none*
29	O praise the Lord, our heav'nly King,	102, 104
30	When all thy mercies, O my God,	71
31	The spacious firmament on high	28
32	The Lord my pasture shall prepare	98
33	All-glorious God, what hymns of praise	10, 99
34	Salvation doth to God belong;	12
35	To God, our never-failing throne	V
36	Before Jehovah's awful throne	30
37	From all that dwell below the skies,	*none*
38	Happy the man, whose hopes rely	*none*
39	Begin the high celestial strain,	*none*
40	Thou turnest man, O Lord, to dust,	41, 55?
41	Hark! from the tomb a doleful sound!	*none*
42	Hark! my gay friend, that solemn toll	*none*
43	Behold the path which mortals tread	*none*
44	Death calls our friends, our neighbors hence	*none*

Hymn No.	First Line	Set at Eckhard No.
45	Vital spark of heav'nly flame!	i
46	Arise, my soul! with rapture rise!	*none*
47	With fervent hearts let all unite,	100

Gloria Patri:	First: To Father, Son, and Holy Ghost	*none*
	Second: To Father, Son, and Holy Ghost	106
	Third: Praise God, from whom all blessings flow	iii
	Fourth: To Father, Son, and Holy Ghost	*none*
	Fifth: To God the Father, Son	*none*
	Sixth: To God the Father, Son	*none*
	Seventh: By Angels in Heav'n	*none*
	Eighth: Sing we to our God above	87
	Ninth: Father, Son, and Holy Ghost	*none*
	Tenth: All glory to our triune God	*none*

Metrical Index of Tunes

Note: Eckhard arranged the numbered tunes (1–85) systematically by meter: Long Meter, Common Meter, Short Meter, and Miscellaneous Meters. The only irregularities in the system are No. 29, which Eckhard included with two L. M. hymns also in special settings, and the last three tunes: 83 and 84 were evidently added as L. M. tunes after the space allotted for that meter had been filled and 85 was fitted in at the end of the C. M. tunes and a number was supplied for it later. (*Pentonville* may have been fitted in at the end of the S. M. tunes after 76 with no number supplied; it is possible that a number "86A" would more nearly represent Eckhard's intention than the one now given to it, 76A.) The unnumbered tunes are arranged generally on the basis of the numbers of the psalms and hymns to which they are set and without regard to their meters. The tune numbers are set in italics, and the page numbers in roman.

Alphabetical Index of Tunes

Note: Tunes taking their names from psalm or hymn numbers are listed in numerical order under Psalm or Hymn. Tune Nos. 80, 97, 98, 101, 103, and 111 have no names. The tune numbers are set in italics, and the page numbers in roman.

Jacob Eckhard's Choirmaster's Book of 1809

Composition, photoengraving, printing, and binding by Kingsport Press, Inc. Text composed in Linotype Granjon; the display type is Goudy Old Style. The facsimile of the choirmaster's book was reproduced from line engravings with a 20 percent mechanical screen added. Printed by offset lithography on 70 lb. Glatfelter's Offset paper. Bound in Holliston's Lexotone. Designed by Robert L. Nance.